Why vo

Rachel Reeves

with a foreword by Gordon Brown

First published in Great Britain in 2010 by
Biteback Publishing Ltd
Heal House
375 Kennington Lane
London
SE11 5QY

ISBN 978-1-84954-019-3

10 9 8 7 6 5 4 3 2 1

A CIP catalogue record for this book is available from the British Library.

Set in Garamond by SoapBox – www.soapboxcommunications.co.uk
Printed and bound in Great Britain by CPI Cox & Wyman, Reading, RG1 8EX

Contents

About the author

Rachel Reeves is Labour's parliamentary candidate in Leeds West. She has been a member of the Labour Party since she was seventeen.

Rachel has spent most of her career at the Bank of England as an economist. From 2000 to 2002 she was in the International Division, covering Japan & China and then the USA. Between 2002 and 2003 Rachel was on secondment to the British embassy in Washington, where she reported and advised on economic policy. On returning to the Bank, Rachel worked in the Corporate team, focusing on productivity, investment and R&D. From 2006 to 2009 Rachel worked for Halifax Bank of Scotland in Yorkshire.

Rachel has published numerous articles and papers on economics and finance, including *Building a Better Balanced UK Economy*, published by the Institute for Public Policy Research, a paper on central bank communication published by the *European Journal on Political Economy*, and an article arguing for quantitative easing for the Fabian Society in December 2008. She has recently also edited *The Road to Copenhagen: The Progressive Case for Climate Action*, published by the Socialist Environment and Resources Association.

Rachel is now a trustee at two local charities, Barca-Leeds and the Leeds Healthy Living Network, both of which work with people in deprived communities offering drug treatment, family support, counselling, youth clubs, cookery classes, health advice and much more. Rachel is also a governor at a local primary school.

Rachel has a Master's degree in economics from the LSE (2004) and a BA in philosophy, politics and economics from New College, Oxford (2000).

Foreword

Times of great challenge mean choices of great consequence and this year our country confronts the biggest choice for a generation. As Rachel makes clear in this book, it is not simply a choice between two parties, but between two radically different directions for our country.

The Conservatives have said that this decade must be 'an age of austerity', but I would argue this is too great a country with too much potential to ever settle for such small ambitions. I believe that the coming decade can be an age not of austerity but of shared prosperity, a progressive decade for a country that is stronger, fairer and more green. Neither outcome is inevitable; it's about the change we choose.

Choices through the recession

In the last eighteen months we have had to confront the biggest economic choices the world has faced since the 1930s and, through the recession, Labour made our choice – we chose to take action.

When faced with the choice of whether markets left to themselves could sort out the crisis or whether governments had to act, we nationalised Northern Rock and took shares in British banks, and as a result not one British saver has lost a single penny. That wasn't inevitable – it was the change we chose.

When faced with the choice between letting the recession run its course or stimulating the economy back to growth, we decided to act, with help for small businesses, targeted tax cuts for millions and advancing our investment in roads, rail and education. That wasn't inevitable – it was the change we chose.

When faced with the choice between accepting unemployment as a price worth paying, or protecting people's livelihoods, we made our choice, and invested in supporting jobs, so that the rate of job losses in this recession has been four times less than if the experience of the early 1990s had been repeated. Even in today's difficult economic climate there are twenty-nine million people in work – two million more men and women providing for their families than in 1997. That wasn't inevitable – it was the change we chose.

When faced with the choice of whether to do nothing as repossessions rose or save the family homes people have worked so hard to buy, we chose to act and 200,000 homeowners were given direct government support to stay in their home. That wasn't inevitable – it was the change we chose.

And when faced with the choice of going our own way or acting with other countries we picked internationalism over isolationism, leading the G20 to a global deal that will save fifteen million jobs. That wasn't inevitable – it was the change we chose.

So never let anybody tell you there is no real difference between the parties. Everything we chose to do to protect people on middle and modest incomes during this recession the Conservatives opposed. Never forget the homes that have been saved, the jobs, the businesses, the hopes, the futures. We did it because we believe in government being on people's side, not passing by on the other side. We did it because we know that great change comes not by accident, but through action.

Choices for the future

Labour's handling of the recession shows that we will always fight for Britain's mainstream majority, the people who do their best and do their bit, and want nothing more than a little support to achieve their dreams. Whether your aspirations are to own your own home, start a business, or make a difference to your neighbourhood, Labour will be fighting for you. That's why I say we are not a party *in* Britain, but the party *of* Britain, because we are on your side wherever you've come from in life and wherever you want to get to in life.

People today have high ambitions for themselves and their families, and it is a strong economy that will be the springboard for people to soar from. The financial crisis has changed everything, and only a party which can draw its lessons will be able to secure Britain's future growth. Labour's new economic model is founded on three guiding principles. That in future finance must always be the servant of people and industry and not their master. That our future economy must be low carbon with a high proportion of skilled green jobs. And that we must realise all of Britain's talent if we are to lead and succeed in a world where most of the new jobs are in the creative, knowledge, service and advanced manufacturing industries.

If we maintain our ruthless focus on those economic priorities, we can unleash a wave of social mobility not seen in this country since the Second World War. If the country chooses the change on offer from Labour, we can not only secure the recovery which the Conservatives would put at risk, but make of it the beginning of a new era for our nation, where every single person can rise as far and as fast as their talents will take them. We will not focus on social mobility *instead* of social justice, but because social mobility *is* social justice.

Britain faces a pivotal moment in its history; the decisions we take today will define the opportunities of a generation. And so as you read this excellent book with its detail on so many different policy areas it is worth always returning to the fundamental question: with which party is my family more likely to get on and not just get by, in whose hands is Britain like to go forwards not back? I believe that the answer is Labour, the party of fairness and of the future.

Labour historically has been at its best when it has projected a strong message about the future of the country – just think of 1945, 1964 or 1997. And so we must always be the party of change – not simply running on our record, but being candid about the future.

So we must be clear: there will be tough decisions to be made about what Britain can afford. To pay for our schools, hospitals, police and the change we want to make, we have to make choices about taxation and public spending. But let no one be in any doubt: as a result of Labour's economic management, Britain started the downturn with the second lowest debt of any G7 economy. And just as we have always taken the hard and tough decisions on stability in the past, we will continue to apply the same rigour to our decisions in the future. We will cut the deficit in half over four years, and we will always be honest with you. That's why every single pledge we make comes with a price tag attached and a clear plan for how that cost will be met. We will protect frontline spending on schools, the NHS, Sure Start and the police because we believe that is the right thing to do, but we will make savings so that we can afford to protect the services the mainstream majority rely on.

So we have announced that we will raise tax at the very top, make cuts in low priority areas, have realistic public sector pay settlements, make efficiency savings and put an extra penny on National Insurance next year so that each and every year we protect and improve Britain's frontline services.

Our opponents would take a very different approach. They want to cut spending now just as they wanted to cut spending all through the recession – regardless of the impact on families and on jobs. They are committed to a giveaway of £200,000 on average to the 3,000 wealthiest estates, at the same time as they threaten cuts to child tax credits and child trust funds for those on modest incomes. And they want to take an indiscriminate axe to frontline services which are used not simply by the poorest but Britain's middle class too. These are not cuts they would make because they have to –

these are the cuts they are making because they want to. It is not inevitable – it is the change they choose.

Conclusion

The last eighteen months will be studied by our children and our children's children – as a time the world was spun on its axis and old certainties were turned on their heads. Each generation believes it is living through changes their parents could never have imagined – but with the collapse of banks, the credit crunch, the trebling of oil prices, the speed of technology and the rise of Asia – nobody now can be in any doubt that we are in a different world. In truth, we haven't seen anything this big since the Industrial Revolution.

So we are not seeking a fourth term in the old age – but to win what will be the first British election of a new global age.

In every time of profound change those with great wealth and privilege have always been able to look after themselves. But Labour's duty, what gives us moral purpose, is serving Britain's majority on middle and modest incomes who need to know that they are not on their own amidst this change, because we are on their side.

And so I hope that you will read this book and think carefully about the big decisions facing us all. Because the choice is real. The consequences are real. The risk is real.

In the pages which follow, you can read a highly personal account of why one Labour supporter and candidate – Rachel Reeves – thinks the country should go forwards with Labour and not backwards with the Conservatives. The stakes are high but, as this book makes abundantly clear: Labour is backing Britain's aspirations, and we're fighting to win.

Gordon Brown
February 2010

Introduction

I went to school in South London. When I was at primary school in the 1980s music teaching was being phased out, special needs teaching was slashed and school trips were cut to save money. At secondary school our library was converted into a classroom and our school sixth form was two pre-fabricated huts in the playground. It meant that there was no place to sit and think and read and study. Despite the fact that we desperately needed more space there was no investment. Those of us who did well did so because of fantastic, dedicated teachers at our school but we succeeded against the odds. We lacked the resources for everyone to have a fair chance.

Over time I realised that what happened when I was at school was not good enough and that everyone should be able to access an excellent education, regardless of background or money. I believed then, and believe today, that everyone should have the opportunity and support to reach their potential and fulfil their ambitions. There are many talented musicians, scientists, engineers and writers out there who never had the chance to develop their skills because they didn't get the support they needed at home or at school. This is a tragic waste of individual talent and a profligate squandering of our national assets. In the increasingly competitive global economy, our future prosperity depends on nurturing and valuing everyone's talents.

But, whether everyone does have those opportunities is not a matter of chance, it is a political choice – a choice about investment in schools and skills, a choice about what sort of state and what sort of society we want. In 1997 Labour was elected on a platform of 'education, education, education' and a broader commitment to reform and invest in our public infrastructure and services.

All around us we can see the results. In Leeds West, where I am standing for Parliament, every primary school has been either re-built or refurbished since 1997. Two new high schools opened their doors in September – one of them an academy for performing arts. Thousands of families, children and pensioners have been lifted out of poverty with the working and pension tax credits and the National Minimum Wage. The standard of social housing has increased as the backlog of repairs inherited in 1997 has been carried out and we have two new district health centres offering out-patient treatment in the community.

Leeds West is not unique in this respect, and across the country we can see the evidence and impact of Labour investment and reform. My old secondary school is now a specialist college in design and technology, with new buildings, state of the art science labs and the latest technologies. The change sends out a message – education matters, and it matters for every child, not just a privileged few. For three successive elections Labour has promised and delivered investment in public services and that investment has helped create an environment in which people can thrive and flourish.

I believe passionately that we need excellent public services – schools, hospitals, parks, housing, museums and transport – for people to achieve their potential. Investment in public services and lifting people out of poverty contribute to a stronger, fairer, more successful society.

A mark of a decent society is one where, whatever circumstances you are born into, you have the opportunity to fulfil your ambitions and aspirations. A decent society is one where really basic things, like access to a good school or a short waiting list at the local hospital, don't depend on how much money you have. A decent society is one where we recognise our collective responsibilities to each other, not just our individual interests. And a society built like that will be better, more cohesive and more successful.

But it is a society we must build together – recognising that markets and the pursuit of our own interests must be tempered with the recognition that everyone deserves decent life chances. This should be backed up by government and institutions to support our shared ambitions and objectives, ensuring that everyone has the opportunity and capacity to make the most of their lives.

The Labour Party was created in 1900 to give working people a say in how the country is governed. Keir Hardie, Labour's first leader, campaigned for a minimum wage and rights for workers. Since 1900, Labour has only been in power for 33 of those 110 years, but has a lot to be proud of. The 1945 government of Clement Attlee created the NHS and the welfare state. The Labour government of the 1960s legalised abortion and homosexuality, introduced the Race Relations Act, expanded comprehensive education and set up the Open University. And from 1997 Labour has realised Keir Hardie's vision of a National Minimum Wage, doubled spending on the NHS and created thousands of Sure Start Children's Centres across the UK. Britain today is also a more democratic country and since 1997 has completed some of the reforms that Keir Hardie passionately wanted to see, with a Scottish Parliament, assemblies in Wales and Northern Ireland and the abolition of the hereditary principle in the House of Lords.

But I know that after thirteen years in power, people have frustrations – frustrations that mistakes have been made, that sometimes the government did not move fast enough or far enough. I accept and understand those frustrations, but ask that the record be considered as a whole and that even when you don't agree with everything, look back to the 1980s and early 1990s and consider whether things have got better or worse – whether Britain today is fairer, whether our schools and hospitals are better and whether there are more opportunities now than there were in 1997. I believe Britain has got better under Labour.

In this book I reflect on the past and look to the future. The challenges we face today are very different, but no less urgent, than those we faced back in 1997. Back then climate change was tucked away in the manifestos of all the main political parties. We have been confronted by the challenges of international terrorism, religious extremism and nuclear proliferation since then, and in 1997 we thought nationalisation of the commanding heights of the economy had been replaced forever with a new vision of the stakeholder economy. Our schools and hospitals have been transformed through investment, but as times move on we must rise to new challenges.

What the recession has taught us is that markets, left to their own devices, will serve sectional interests and not the public interest. But through regulation, taxation and subsidies we can mould the market economy to serve our collective interests. While Conservatives believe that government should get out of the way – scale back regulation – Labour believes that without an active and supportive government, the worst excesses of markets will lead to future crises that could eclipse the recession we are now emerging from.

We must, as we emerge from recession, re-structure our economy so that it serves people and not just profits. This requires an economy based on a broader range of industries, one where the financial sector recognises its responsibilities and is better regulated, and one where we invest in the skills, jobs and industries of the future including in green technologies and manufacturing.

This election is one of those crucial elections – like 1945, which created the welfare state, 1979, which re-structured the economy or 1997, which transformed public services. The direction of the nation is at stake. As in those elections, the main two parties today, Labour and Conservative, have very different conceptions about the role of government, how to respond to the recession and the path back to growth.

We are the first generation confronted with the challenge of averting catastrophic climate change. Left unchecked, markets will not deliver the outcomes that are required, whether it is reductions in emissions, financing new technologies, or supporting poorer countries in adapting to new realities. It doesn't matter to markets whether they leave environmental degradation in their wake, if the economic transactions today harm the planet for future generations or if the world's poorest people pay the highest price for our consumption of the world's resources. But it matters to us. Like the challenges that have come before, Labour will approach climate change from a perspective of international co-operation and a recognition that markets do not have all the solutions. We need a legally binding treaty on climate change and the next few years are critical in terms of implementing any deal. A fourth-term Labour government would prioritise this global challenge.

The nature of the challenges we face makes us increasingly aware that we require international answers. Just and sustainable solutions to the challenges of global warming mean recognising the impact of the policies and lifestyles in one country on the most vulnerable communities and countries. The challenges we face in relation to fixing the global economy similarly require global solutions. Regulation in one country will not do the trick – banks are internationally mobile, as we have seen through the credit crunch.

Globalisation will only intensify in the coming years. Through trade, financial flows, migration and information technology, challenges, threats and opportunities will increasingly disregard national borders. To keep pace, we need to find new solutions in the emerging political, economic and social landscape.

Labour has always been a party international in its perspective. Today, that is most evident through engagement in Europe and through leadership in pushing the Millennium Development Goals to ensure justice for developing economies. The Conservatives' refusal to engage in Europe would damage Britain's capacity to lead the debate on financial regulation and the environment and hence the ability to influence issues that will have enormous impact at home. When the challenges we face are increasingly global in reach it is more important than ever that Britain is governed by a party that takes its international obligations, and its international potential, seriously, and is determined to operate at the heart of institutions like the EU, the United Nations and G20.

The economic and political challenges that the global, financial and climate change crises have presented are formidable but they are not ones that Labour has been cowed by. They pose new tests that every party must address and that every voter must consider as the election approaches.

This means new politics, not business as usual. New policies to move Britain forward after the economic crisis and new policies to ensure that a low carbon economy is at the heart of everything we do. The sort of recovery we build is up to us. At its best we will build a more diverse economy, better regulated, with more choice for consumers, an extension of opportunities and skills, more responsive public services and a more sustainable economy so that we can pass on to our children a safe and secure planet.

In the new economy we must unleash the potential of all our citizens, allowing everyone to aim high and achieve their ambitions. This challenge has intensified over the last decade as the scope and potential of jobs to migrate abroad has increased. The emergence of economies like China and India on the world stage makes it imperative that all our young people leave school with the skills and qualifications they need to succeed. As more jobs will require high skills, it is important that high skills are not the preserve of only a well-educated elite but something we all can access and aspire to.

If we waste the potential of any young person we squander their talents and Britain's resources. So, investment in apprenticeships, expanding the number of university places, more intensive one-to-one tuition in our schools and an emphasis on learning beyond school are essential for our future economic success. While business recognises the importance of skills, businesses do not have to keep jobs in the UK, and so there is a critical role for government in ensuring that Britain is a high-skilled competitive economy, unleashing the talents of all.

And in uncertain and changing times, we value strong communities more. Neighbourhoods with a sense of identity, free from crime and anti-social behaviour and where we feel safe and secure, will support us and our families against a background of change. Strong institutions, like the NHS, local democracy, neighbourhood policing teams, community groups, youth clubs and religious groups, all add to our sense of belonging and place. And they all reflect the fact that we are not atomised individuals but part of a wider community and society which shapes our identity, values and sense of self. These voluntary networks – backed up by effective institutions and an enabling state – are crucial in an uncertain world to help us achieve our potential and to provide the safety net and support we need in difficult times.

What Labour stands for is a politics of community, a belief that we are all in it together, that society is a matter of shared obligations and mutual responsibilities. We believe society will be stronger if it includes rather than excludes, that individuals thrive best in a supportive and cohesive community and that we can achieve more collectively than we could hope to secure individually. It is because of those values that I believe Labour is the right party to deliver a fairer, more sustainable and responsible economy and society.

The choice at this election is between two fundamentally different visions of Britain. It's not just a choice of personalities or even who's going to be a better manager of the system. And it's not about change versus the status quo. It's about what kind of change you want – and what kind of Britain you want to see. It's about whether you are optimistic about Britain's future and the possibilities ahead or pessimistic – believing instead that Britain is somehow broken and unable to adapt to the new challenges we are faced with. Labour offers change, change to support families on modest and middle incomes and hope for a future of aspirations fulfilled.

The focus of this book is the economy – because building a stronger, more responsible and fairer economy is at the heart of everything we must do. So, chapter one sets out a vision of jobs for the future – including green technologies, investment in skills and strong regional economies. Underpinning jobs we need a strong and fair economy, so chapter two sets out how we can reduce the budget deficit in a fair and responsible way and how to ensure that banks are not allowed to go back to their old ways, but instead are effectively and robustly regulated. Building on that, chapter three sets out how to expand opportunities, providing everyone with the support they need to get a job and progress at work, with training, tax credits, the minimum wage and affordable childcare. At the heart of the new economy is a low carbon future – with collective global action to tackle this most important challenge, and this is set out in chapter four. Increasingly the challenges we face are international – not least on the economy, alleviating poverty and climate change, so in chapter five I set our Britain's role in the world. Despite the economic challenges we face, we must continue to transfer power to parents, pupils, and patients as we deliver 21st-century public services – in fact that is crucial to unleashing the talents of everyone so we can compete and prosper in the global economy. So chapter six looks at education reform and chapter seven at health reform. But the ability to fulfil your potential and build a fairer, stronger

Britain also requires us to do more to tackle poverty and inequalities – because it is morally right to do so, and because it makes practical sense too. Chapter eight looks at how poverty is preventable. Politics and policy is felt, ultimately, in our communities – where we live and work. In uncertain times, strong communities matter most and so chapter nine looks at how Labour is building stronger, more cohesive and secure communities.

Beyond policies, a new politics is demanded, and in the wake of the expenses saga, people rightly demand a reformed politics to restore trust and integrity. Unless people engage with politics it will be impossible to secure the change we need especially because, as I have set out, the challenges we face require an agile and enabling state, working with individuals, families, businesses and communities to unleash talent. So, as someone standing to become a Member of Parliament, I will end the book with a reflection on how to restore trust.

This short book is not a manifesto. It offers my own reasons for voting Labour. And because devolution means that Scotland, Wales and Northern Ireland now, quite rightly, have more power over their own affairs, the discussion of public services focuses on what has happened in England. There are also some personal stories from people's own experiences which tell a stronger story than statistics could ever hope to.

This book is an account of what Labour has achieved, because I am proud of those achievements. But it also sets out our future challenges and what it is about Labour's values that will help us build a fairer and more just society. I hope it will compel and persuade you, the reader, to vote Labour.

Jobs for the future

I joined the Labour Party as I grew up under the Thatcher government. Greed and individualism prevailed. Some prospered but many people lost their jobs and their homes – the Tories just left them to struggle. Labour offered a new vision, 'for the many, not the few'.

NANCY PLATTS, LABOUR PARLIAMENTARY CANDIDATE
FOR BRIGHTON PAVILION

A sustainable recovery

The recession has hit British families and businesses hard. Many people have lost their jobs, or are worried that they might; previously successful businesses have struggled to get the finance they need; and some families have struggled to pay their mortgage. Understanding the causes of the crisis, responding to the recession and building the jobs of the future are the key challenges of the next government – and with Labour we will build a different, more sustainable economy.

The recession has been very tough, the worst global downturn in sixty years. But it has been different from the recessions of the 1980s and 1990s. Unlike the approach of the Conservative governments back then, this Labour government has done all that it can to support the economy and jobs, limiting redundancies, business closures and home repossessions. It has been the right thing to do – supporting families and businesses who had no responsibility for the financial crisis they have had to cope with. And it is the right economic approach too, helping to build the recovery, and avoiding writing off a generation of people to unemployment and economic inactivity, as happened in the past. Labour has learnt from the mistakes of the 1980s and 1990s but also from the mistakes of the last decade – where insufficient regulation – at home and abroad – allowed the financial sector to make irresponsible decisions and take excessive risks which almost brought the world economy to its knees.

We must now look towards the future – to what sort of economy and jobs we want to build in the wake of the financial crisis, because what we do today will lay the foundations for our future economic success. The role of government is to support the economy through the recovery, to enable people to succeed and fulfil their potential, and to build the jobs of the future.

The recession has shown the need for a more strategic, agile and collective response from government – for, as we have seen, markets acting alone will not serve our collective interests. The reality is that it will take government, working with businesses, to build the strong, fair and competitive economy that is in all our interests. That is the Labour approach.

The Conservative Party's ideological hostility to such a role for government has seen them oppose the measures taken by Labour to support jobs through the recession, and leaves them without credible answers to the questions of how we build growth and jobs in challenging circumstances.

The state and the market

Until the 1980s, under Labour and Conservative governments, the UK pursued a corporatist economic policy – a policy of national champions, with some successes but also with costly mistakes. This changed in the 1980s when there began two decades of embracing the free market – in the economy and society – including the privatisation of many public services. While New Labour accepted a lot of the changes, it also recognised that an approach that relied solely on market forces neglected important things that markets alone cannot provide – like infrastructure, skills and research and development (R&D). Some things needed to be changed. So from 1997, Labour doubled spending on R&D, tripled the number of apprenticeships, strengthened links between businesses and universities, and regenerated our towns and cities.

But while Labour recognised that the market alone cannot provide the public services and infrastructure we need, what none of the political parties here or abroad foresaw – including the Labour government – was that the financial services sector was expanding in an unsustainable way and that the economy was becoming overly reliant on financial services for jobs, growth and tax revenues.

While Labour has no ambition to do down or undermine financial services, it does want to see other parts of the economy grow and prosper. Labour wants to build a stronger, more balanced and sustainable economy for the future.

We need, in the wake of the financial crisis, a broader-based, more responsible capitalism with a government that understands that markets cannot function in a moral vacuum, and that strong institutions are needed to ensure that it is not the poorest who pay the highest price for the recession – especially as they are least responsible for what markets throw at them. We need a remodelled economy based on values of fairness and opportunity to meet the challenges of this century.

The opportunity economy

The Labour Party is guided by a passion to build and promote a just, fair and prosperous society – where everyone has the chance to fulfil their potential and ambition: the opportunity economy. A society where it is who you are, what effort you put in, and what skills you develop that determines the reward that you get. The Labour Party believes that everyone should be able to shape their own life, rather than circumstances shaping it for them. And this makes economic sense too. If we waste the talents of just one person then we lose their contribution to our shared future prosperity. Central to the opportunity economy are high quality jobs.

Labour in 1997 inherited a Conservative legacy where approximately 400,000 people were paid less than £3 an hour and many were paid as little as £1 or £1.50 an hour – especially women and part-time workers. Unemployment had reached three million or above on two occasions, with a lost generation of young unemployed. If you wanted to improve your pay and conditions you might have considered joining a trade union. But, under legislation introduced by Margaret Thatcher, you could have lost your job just by being a member.

Since 1997, Labour has supported working people through the introduction of the National Minimum Wage that Keir Hardie first campaigned for, the New Deal for long-term and youth unemployment, working and child tax credits, and maternity and paternity leave. Many lives transformed – expanding opportunities so we can all develop our potential.

Peter, Leeds

I left school in 1984 when I was seventeen and couldn't get a job. I went to college and did courses in gardening and light engineering, but with mass unemployment there were very few jobs to be had, so it was impossible to get started. I even did unpaid work experience, but I had no real support to get work.

Then Labour got in and brought in the New Deal. There was a lot of training over several months to prepare us for working and to give us all the skills we needed. I passed all of the courses – some with 100 per cent – and got my first full-time job in 1999 at the age of thirty-three. I wouldn't ever want to go back to being unemployed.

Support through the recession

The recession that started in America, but spread with a vengeance across the world, revealed weaknesses in the way our economy evolved. An over-reliance on the financial sector and high levels of consumer debt financed by a housing bubble resulted in a deep recession which we are only just emerging from. The Labour government reacted swiftly in response to the downturn, helping to avoid a recession becoming a depression. But going forward things must change.

Labour's policies mean around 500,000 fewer people have lost their jobs than had been predicted at the start of the recession. Writing in *The Observer*, Will Hutton emphasised the difference Labour has made:

> [The government] has poured resources into the Jobcentre Plus network to increase its capacity... 55 per cent of new [unemployment benefit] claimants are leaving the register within three months and 73 per cent within six months – only fractionally lower than in normal times. There has been the £1 billion Future Jobs Fund, and then the guarantee that every 18–24-year-old receiving Jobseekers Allowance will get a job or training after six months. In total, £5 billion has been spent – and it is working.

These measures, along with reduced tax revenues and higher spending on benefits and public services, have increased the budget deficit. But, without them, more people would have lost their jobs, more businesses would have folded and more families would have lost their homes. Collectively, we would be enduring a longer and more severe recession as workers would lose skills, the economy would lose productive businesses, and we would be paying more out to support people out of work and business.

Through the downturn, David Cameron and George Osborne have opposed every single measure that Labour has taken, including the job guarantee for young people and support for businesses to keep people in work or training.

Unlike the Conservatives, Labour will not under-estimate the scale of the challenge, or the role for government, in helping build a strong economy again.

A new industrial strategy

Labour has learnt important lessons from the recession. The financial crisis has shown us that we need a broader-based economy and that to do this we need to support the growth of new industries and jobs. The role of government is not limited to addressing crises. It can, and should, continue to support the economy. Without a government that works with businesses, we risk losing out as other countries actively invest in their industrial strengths, especially when economies like China pursue an aggressive expansion of their industrial and technology-based sectors.

If UK companies are to compete in new technologies with the best producers in the world, then we must identify and pursue the policies that will support businesses and draw the benefits from markets to get the jobs of the future that we need.

The real risk is that a Conservative government, with its small-government mantra, will condemn British families and businesses to economic stagnation at this crucial turning point in the economy.

Returning to full employment depends on a new industrial strategy, with investment in skills; encouraging research and development; a green new deal; an entrepreneurial and enterprising culture; and a regionally diversified economic strategy.

It is not inevitable that we return to strong economic growth, and without the right decisions we will lose opportunities and jobs for a generation. A strong economy with opportunities for all to succeed will not develop by chance.

Investing in skills and training

Education and skills give us the opportunities to fulfil our potential. The jobs of the future will increasingly require high levels of skills and training as we compete internationally for business. That is why Labour is upskilling the workforce with apprenticeships, diplomas and better access to training in the workplace.

The industries of the future – including modern manufacturing, digital technologies, creative industries and pharmaceuticals – require high level skills in science, technology, engineering and maths. These are also crucial to the success of green technologies which have the potential to create thousands more jobs.

I can see the difference that Labour's investment in skills is making in Leeds. In the last ten years, the number of young people graduating with apprenticeships has increased sharply and at Leeds College of Building over 400 young people started an apprenticeship this year, enabling the college to expand and offer more courses for the next generation of builders, architects, plumbers and joiners.

Labour is ambitious for everyone, with a commitment that three quarters of young people will be able to participate in higher education or complete an advanced apprenticeship by the age of thirty. On top of this, Labour is creating 35,000 advanced apprenticeship opportunities, to produce the skilled technicians for the future. These new engineers will lay the cables that will expand access to high speed internet, while new technicians will build the new electric cars and wind turbines of the future.

But, we must also ensure that we are helping people already in work – particularly those who did not get the chance of a good education the first time round. Schemes like Train to Gain and Union Learning Representatives are helping upskill the workforce so that everyone can take part in the new opportunity economy. Labour wants everyone to have a good job, and for people to know that their children and grandchildren will get the skills and qualifications to get a good job too.

High quality jobs, where we can expect a fair wage for the effort we put in, are things that mark out a successful economy and a decent society. Labour is committed to achieving them.

But while the UK is increasingly moving to a high-skill economy, there will also be more jobs in care industries, to support an ageing population. For these jobs too, we must ensure that everyone has the training to do them well and is offered the chance to change careers or move up the ladder at work. And whatever you want to achieve, and wherever you have got to in life, Labour will ensure fair pay and protection in the workplace (I will return to that in chapter three).

In contrast to Labour's investment in skills for everyone, the Conservatives oppose Labour's promise that everyone should be able to continue in education or training up until the age of eighteen. Not only would this approach damage the prospects of people, particularly from working-class families and communities, but it would threaten the competitiveness of our economy, which increasingly depends on the talents of us all.

As the global economy gets more competitive, we must redouble our efforts to ensure that everyone – at school, college, university and the workplace – gets the opportunity to play their full role in the new economy and fulfil their aspirations and ambitions.

Innovation economy

To develop the jobs of the future we need businesses that innovate and utilise the latest technologies to meet new challenges – including the climate change challenge.

Already, £4 billion of tax credits have supported research and development, while Innovation Vouchers are encouraging businesses and universities to work together to develop technologies and ideas for future businesses and jobs. Government support for universities to spin out new technologies, as well as a doubling of government investment in science, are ensuring that, under Labour, Britain is at the cutting edge of science and innovation.

The importance of tax credits for helping fund research reflects the fact that investing in new ideas is expensive and high risk and benefits the whole economy, not just the business or individual who pays for or carries out the research. No sector acting alone will deliver the strategic focus that we need to build the dynamic and competitive businesses of the future, and markets do not always deliver the optimal outcomes. Working together – government, business and universities – we can often achieve more and bring benefits across the whole economy.

But enterprising and innovative businesses require more than ideas – they need investment to grow. The UK financial markets have historically not served some growing British companies well and the credit crisis has exacerbated this problem by dramatically reducing the appetite for risk. We need to keep up pressure on banks to lend, but Labour is also looking for wider solutions to more structural problems, with the public and private sectors working together to support innovative businesses.

That is why in the last year Labour has created the Strategic Investment Fund, worth nearly £1 billion. The money will target businesses that need funding to test and experiment with new technologies – often working with universities to do so. And because every part of Britain has entrepreneurs and innovative ideas, the fund will include regional pots of money to ensure that great ideas – wherever they are – can get off the ground. The Conservatives want to reduce corporation tax by cutting vital business investment allowances – but this is short sighted: unless we invest in the industries of the future we will not have the business success or growth we need.

At a turning point in the economic cycle, as we are facing now, innovation is more important than ever – it is new ideas and new ways of doing things that can spur the industries of the future.

Green jobs

No sector depends more on innovation and skills than the green technology industries. Almost 900,000 people in the UK already work in the green, or low carbon, sector and in the supply chains supporting it – not just in green manufacturing but in green services like consultancy or low carbon venture capital and in traditional building industries like insulation and fitting. The sector has been growing, even through the recession. We must now ensure that we have the infrastructure and framework to take advantage of new opportunities – as the government's New Industry, New Jobs strategy, led by Business Secretary Peter Mandelson, sets out.

Labour is taking the strategic approach, leading the modernisation of the economy. We know that businesses will not invest in change and individuals will not make the shift to more environmental goods and services unless they believe that is the direction the economy is going in and if there are the right incentives for them to do so. Clear leadership, and firm commitments by government – for example on nuclear and renewable energy – will unlock billions of pounds of investment. We need to maintain momentum and clear strategic direction through all the actions of government to get the investment and jobs that green industries have the potential to bring.

Because Labour recognises that markets do not have all the answers, government must help drive forward the transition to a more sustainable, greener economy. That means increasing the price of carbon so that business invests in renewable energy. It also means using public sector procurement to increase demand for low carbon goods and services, including low carbon cars. The transition also requires investment in our infrastructure, like the National Grid, which must increasingly support low carbon industry. And it requires entrepreneurs having access to finance so that they can build the technologies of the future, including a £2 billion programme of investment in UK innovation by the Technology Strategy Board.

There is huge potential for our green new deal to benefit every region in the UK. The North East, for example, could gain from wind energy generation by utilising existing offshore infrastructure, skills and technologies established by the oil and gas industry. The European Commission is also supporting South Yorkshire's bid for carbon capture and storage – demonstrating the economic importance of placing ourselves at the centre of Europe.

Greening the economy must be at the centre of everything we do. Over a quarter of carbon emissions in the UK come from energy use in our homes, and as the construction industry recovers from recession it must focus on sustainable development, including re-fitting existing buildings and building the low and zero carbon homes of the future. The greening of the UK economy will generate high-tech jobs and create bread and butter jobs in all our communities – fitting new boilers, lagging lofts and insulating walls.

Over the next few years climate change and economic re-structuring offer a unique opportunity to build an economy that is more sustainable for future generations to enjoy.

We must be pragmatic about the role of government and the state, not sceptical about what we can achieve together. If we make the right decisions now we could be a world leader in the green technologies of the future – bringing jobs, investment and skills to the UK.

Supporting enterprise

Entrepreneurs must have incentives to generate new ideas, turn them into businesses and grow their firms.

Small businesses have been challenged through the recession, but government can ensure that a temporary recession does not mean that businesses permanently close or that workers permanently lose their jobs. Despite the recession, there are over one million more businesses than in 2000, and Labour has been determined to support them through the recession. Phil is just one businessman who has managed, with help from government, to come through the recession without laying off a single worker. He is feeling optimistic now about the future.

Phil, Leeds

I have been running a printing business for fifteen years and employ forty-five staff. Like everyone, my business has been hit by the recession – 25–30 per cent of sales have been lost and revenues are down 10 per cent. But, honestly, without the support of government things would have been much worse, and because of the support I've had I've been able to stay afloat, and am optimistic about the future.

I received a grant that allowed me to buy some new equipment, enabling us to bring work in house that was previously outsourced. I have had to cut the hours of some staff, but because of the grant and low interest rates all staff have kept their jobs.

I have used the recession to re-evaluate my business model. I have bought new software, and am currently working with the new local academy to take on an apprentice and support them through college.

The recession has been tough, but with the support of government my business will get through it, stronger than ever.

Entrepreneurs need to be free to create jobs, as it will be the million small choices of the market, supported by the government, that define our future success. That is why our 18 per cent capital gains tax rate is among the lowest in the world and our corporation tax rate among the lowest in the G7. A competitive tax and regulatory environment is also important for businesses and jobs and is something Labour will preserve. But a good place to do business is about more than tax. Government must work strategically with business to ensure stable, strong and steady growth and low inflation, coupled with an industrial strategy which helps businesses access finance, skills and technology, and so helps them invest in our shared future.

A regionally diversified economy

Although we have faced a global recession, the routes out of it will be local and regional. Every region must have a strategy for re-building and re-balancing its economy, based on local strengths and comparative advantages.

In Yorkshire, we take huge pride in our industrial past. From wool, coal and steel, to retail and finance, our industries have powered the nation and enriched the region. As we plan for the recovery we need to build a future of which we can be equally proud. So must every region of Britain.

One of the most invidious effects of the recessions of the 1980s and 1990s was to rob communities of the sense that they could build a better future for themselves. The true test of the success of our local economic strategies today will be whether, as the economy recovers, they can return to local people a true sense of control over their own economic future. It was to give this autonomy and power that Tony Blair and John Prescott set up the Regional Development Agencies (RDAs) in 1999, promoting enterprise and driving economic growth in every region. The RDAs have been a success. An independent study by PricewaterhouseCoopers in 2009, showed that, on average, every £1 spent by the RDAs generates an extra £4.50 of economic output for their regional economies. Not a bad rate of return by anyone's reckoning.

RDAs can support the economy in a way that Whitehall never

could. They are closer to the businesses they help, and so better able to meet their needs.

The economy is at a turning point, and the policies we pursue today will shape the economies and communities of the future. To scrap the RDAs, as the Conservatives propose, would rob the regions of the UK of the opportunity to shape their own destiny. Strong regional economies to support local businesses and jobs are essential for thriving, sustainable and proud communities – and that requires regional leadership and vision.

A cohesive and prosperous economy

The sort of economy we build in the wake of the financial crisis is up to us.

Labour's approach is that markets do not have all the answers and can be destabilising, but that micro-managing of business by government is unproductive too. This approach is based on a sense of collective responsibility and the desire to encourage new opportunities. Markets should be given space to function, but they should sit alongside an agile and enabling state that corrects market failures, while empowering and enabling people to make the most of their talents in the new opportunity economy.

A dynamic capitalist economy is not an end in itself but a means to a stronger, more cohesive and prosperous society. An economy that builds for the long term is the economy that will expand opportunities and realise ambitions – supporting skills, innovation, green jobs and enterprise in all our regions – enabling each and every one of us to shape our own destinies and achieve our potential. This is the economy we need to build for the future, and it is the Labour vision. Whether we choose to build this economy and these jobs, or whether we choose the Conservative approach of letting markets operate in isolation, divorced from our shared needs and objectives, is the real choice that we are presented with at the election.

A strong and fair economy

I joined the Labour Party because it brings together people who individually do not have power but together can and do change society. The Labour Party has been at the heart of virtually every improvement in society in the past century: the emancipation of women, the National Health Service, health and safety protection, the minimum wage, rights for gay men and women, the right to be free of racist abuse, equal pay. All these things have two things in common: we have supported them and the Tories have opposed them.

JOHN CRYER, FORMER MP FOR HORNCHURCH

A more responsible capitalism

To underpin the jobs of the future, we need a strong and fair economy. Britain has great strengths: we are an open economy with excellent trade links; we have some of the best businesses in the world, and a highly skilled and entrepreneurial workforce; and Labour has invested in key public services and infrastructure over the last decade.

However, we must also address the challenges we face. We know that some things need to change: the budget deficit that rose to deal with the recession has to be brought down in a way that does not damage growth; and there must be no return to the massive bonuses and excessive risk taking which came so close to causing a global depression. Labour has learnt lessons – regulation was too light-touch before the financial crisis, and the economy had become too reliant on financial services and consumer spending for growth. We know that a different sort of economy needs to be built.

A more responsible capitalism alongside a more active government: an economy where we recognise that we have mutual responsibilities and commitments, and where we understand that the profit motive alone will not deliver the sort of Britain we want to see.

Gordon Brown recently spoke about Labour's approach to markets. He said:

> We can now see that markets cannot self-regulate, but they can self-destruct and, if untrammelled and unbridled, they can become not just the enemy of the good society; they can become the enemy of the good economy. Markets are in the public interest but they are not synonymous with it.

Government must provide the right framework for growth and job creation, while businesses and banks must remember that they need a strong society as much as a flourishing society needs dynamic businesses.

Through the recession

Labour has sought to protect people in order to ensure that it is not the poorest who pay the highest price for the recession, with measures aimed at supporting families, jobs and small businesses. The VAT cut, increased child benefit, pension credit and winter fuel payments have all helped families and pensioners. And Labour provided support for businesses too, including loan guarantees, tax deferrals and the car and boiler scrappage schemes. Cuts in interest rates and quantitative easing got money into the economy when it was needed most.

Economists agree that the measures have made a difference. We now know that the UK economy is growing again – but that recovery is fragile both here and abroad, and government cannot afford to turn its back now.

David Blanchflower, Professor of Economics, Dartmouth College and the University of Stirling

A year ago I was particularly worried that unemployment would rise to well over three million. Fortunately it is nearer to 2½ million, primarily due to the prompt action of this government. VAT was cut, there was cash for bangers and help was extended to the unemployed in general and to the young unemployed in particular, and these policies seem to have worked. Without this intervention unemployment would certainly have been well above three million by now. We have won the opening battle. The worry is that the war could still be lost.

Obviously accommodative monetary policy has helped, although the Monetary Policy Committee should have cut rates and started quantitative easing sooner.

Action by the Labour government has prevented the economy from falling off a cliff. But the risks of a double-dip recession remain. The similarities to what happened in the US in 1937 are instructive. Tightening policy too soon could potentially be the most serious economic policy error of our lifetimes. The unemployed are watching. Keep the stimulus going.

I recently met a woman whose son had lost his job in a high street shop that closed just before Christmas. He was applying for jobs and receiving huge support from the Jobcentre. He hopes to get another job soon, but also knows that if he is out of work for six months he will get intensive support and a guarantee of a job or the opportunity to re-train. How different, his mother told me, from the early 1980s when her husband had lost his job and the family had lost their home. This story is one of hundreds. No government can fully insulate businesses and families from the impact of a recession. But the decisions made by Labour have meant that all that could have been done has been done.

In fact, we now know that if we had responded to this recession in the way that the Conservatives responded to the recession of the 1990s, employment would have fallen by 1.8 million more than it has. And while Labour has taken this action, helping protect jobs, homeowners and small businesses, the Conservatives have opposed every action taken by the government – retreating to their approach of the past – letting the recession run its course without regard to its toll on families and businesses.

Kelly, Swansea

I am twenty-three and have two young children. My husband, like many others, has been affected by the current economy and has been out of work since May last year. I have worked at the same place for the past six years, part time. During this time in our lives we did not have much to live on and were faced with losing our house, as we did not take out the insurance to cover the payments. The government stepped in and has been paying the interest on our mortgage. Not only do we get this but my income gets topped up with tax credits and child benefit and I pay reduced council tax.

Before my husband lost his job I was attending night college, doing an access course. Although money was tight I did not give up my dream to go to university and do a degree in social policy and criminology. I am now at university and the first in my family to do so. I get good grants and I do not pay to attend. I also receive childcare help which means I don't have to worry about paying for childcare fees, and my husband is still able to keep job hunting.

In addition, my husband is now getting help from the Jobcentre to start up his own business.

So I believe the Labour government has helped me and

---

my family. Without its dedication to our working-class family and those in need of it most, my family and I would have lost everything. I am also grateful that during this economic crisis we have come out on top and are still working up to a better life.

Sound public finances

The cost of supporting families and businesses through the recession with targeted spending increases and tax cuts – alongside the fall in tax receipts caused by the recession – has been an increase in the budget deficit, which will in the financial year 2009/10 be between 12 per cent and 13 per cent of GDP. But, without this support the recession would have been more painful and protracted – and in the long run would have cost the public purse more as the economy would have taken longer to recover. This view is shared by *The Guardian*'s economic commentator Larry Elliot, who wrote in late 2009 that 'deep cuts in interest rates, the £200 billion of electronic money pumped into the economy through quantitative easing and the fast-tracking of public investment prevented this year's plunge in output from being even more severe'.

The UK went into recession with the second lowest debt burden in the G7 – our debt was less than in France, Germany and the United States – and it is lower now, as we emerge from the crisis. Because of that, our actions, as well as being right, are affordable.

We must support the economy, but over time, as the recovery is assured, this extra spending and higher borrowing should be reduced. Government, like the rest of us, must ultimately live within its means. That is why Labour, under Chancellor Alistair Darling, has introduced a fiscal responsibility bill that commits the government to halving the budget deficit in four years. Through a combination of Labour's growth strategy to get the economy moving again, targeted tax increases and cuts to public spending, halving the budget deficit in four years is achievable and credible.

It is essential that these plans are realistic and transparent. The deficit must fall from £178 billion this year to £96 billion in 2013/14. Under Labour, £25 billion will come from growth. But as the Chancellor has set out, £57 billion must come from discretionary action: in other words, decisions. Two thirds of this will be delivered through spending cuts, one third through taxes. On tax, Labour has set out plans to raise £19 billion from new taxes. That leaves £38 billion to be achieved by spending cuts. Here too, Labour has been clear. Capital investment will fall from today's historically unprecedented levels, and departments will have to cut back, including £20 billion of cuts and efficiencies already announced in the pre-Budget report – for example from consultancy, marketing, IT spend and a reduction in top civil service pay.

While Labour has supported the economy through the recession, the Conservatives wanted to reduce spending in the middle of the downturn and this year they would introduce spending cuts while the economic recovery is still fragile.

This approach goes against all the historical evidence – witness the lost decade of growth in Japan in the 1990s as the government there did too little too late, and the American depression in the 1930s. It also goes against everything that world leaders are doing today. As Dominique Strauss-Kahn, managing director of the IMF, said in November 2009, 'we recommend erring on the side of caution, as exiting [from stimulus plans] too early is costlier than exiting too late'. Cutting spending during the downturn is dangerous and risks plunging Britain back into recession. Every country in the world – including the US, China, Australia, France and Germany – has cut taxes and increased spending during the recession. The Conservatives are isolated in their opposition to the measures that have helped protect jobs, businesses and families here in the UK.

But George Osborne is not listening to the evidence. While the Conservatives stick with their siren call – 'cut spending now' and promise an 'age of austerity' which would put the jobs, savings and homes of people on modest and middle incomes at risk, Labour is responsibly working to ensure a strong and sustainable economic recovery.

The other crucial difference between Labour and the Conservatives is how to reduce the deficit when the time is right. While the Conservatives argue that the burden of reducing the deficit should come from spending cuts, Labour believes that taxes should increase for those who can afford it. From April 2010, people earning over £150,000 will pay a marginal rate of tax of 50 per cent. Pensions relief for higher earners will be reduced in order to reduce the deficit in a fair and sustainable way, and a penny will be added to National Insurance to help us maintain frontline services in health, education and policing. Meanwhile, the Conservatives sometimes claim they are opposed to the new top rate of tax, and sometimes say they would keep it.

The tax priorities of the Conservatives are very different: their number one commitment is to raise the inheritance tax threshold to £2 million – a tax cut of £200,000 for the richest 3,000 estates – one of the most regressive, anti-egalitarian tax changes ever proposed. And this proposal is doubly unfair – not just because it helps only the wealthiest 3 per cent of estates, but because it is the rest of us who pay for it.

Or take their married couples tax break – a policy which back in January changed three times in the course of one day. The current Conservative scheme would exclude many parents who both work, and would do nothing for those widowed or divorced. In fact, if a man divorced his wife and then re-married he would take his tax allowance with him, leaving his first wife and children worse off. The pledge would cost £4.9 billion – supposedly to be raised from taxes on other families – but George Osborne cannot give us the details on exactly what this means or how it would be funded. And this is supposed to be a 'flagship' policy which they've been working on for four years.

Under the Conservatives, the highest paid will not be asked to contribute to reducing the budget deficit, so the burden will fall on families with middle and low incomes. Indeed the Conservatives are explicit about taking away support from middle-class families – including abolishing the working tax credit to families earning more than £31,000 and scrapping the child trust fund for children whose parents earn more than £16,000.

Perhaps most worryingly, the Conservatives' numbers simply do not add up. While they talk tough and claim that they will cut the deficit faster and more sharply than Labour, it was exposed in January that they had a £34 billion credibility gap between their spending commitments and tax promises. This does not even include some of their expensive promises that are too vague to cost. A real weakness of David Cameron is that he wants to be liked – by everyone. He promises a tax cut here – for married couples, and another one there – on inheritance tax for the wealthy. And he promises a bit more spending here – on more prison places, and another one there – for more rooms in hospitals. You may agree with some of them and not with others but the point is, you cannot promise, on a nod and a wink, everything to everyone. There are tough decisions to be made in the next few months and years. The public have a right to know what the Conservatives would do if they got elected – and how it would be paid for. At the moment we do not know.

The new economy

Britain is one the best places in the world for starting and growing a new business – and we must ensure that this remains the case, being careful not to make indiscriminate cuts that put our long-term competitiveness at risk.

Charles Allen CBE, broadcaster and businessman

As I travel around the world I meet a lot of businesspeople and entrepreneurs who tell me that Britain is a great place to do business. They talk about our talented and creative workforce and the legislative and regulatory framework. Labour has done a lot to make sure that Britain has the skills, science base and infrastructure to succeed.

The government has also reacted swiftly and effectively to the recession, with a package of measures, including VAT cuts and 'cash for bangers', that helped drive the automotive industry and new policies to get people, particularly young people, back to work quickly. What is critical now is that the government continues to support the recovery.

Whether it is economic policy, regeneration, or social policy, much has been achieved but there is still much to be done. We need to work with the government to finish the job.

We know, however, that in the next few years there will be less government money available. That is why in 2009 Labour created Infrastructure UK to unleash private sector funding for investment in transport, nuclear power, the National Grid and digital infrastructure. Infrastructure UK will bring money from the private sector – including from pension funds – generating a return higher than from government bonds but more secure than from equities, ensuring that Britain continues to invest in its essential infrastructure.

Labour's management of the economy has been focused not only on the conviction that the government has a clear responsibility to build a strong and fair economy, but also on the reciprocal duties owed by banks and businesses to the society where they operate. Labour will continue to support hard-working families and businesses, while requiring that everyone – including the banks – plays by the rules.

Reform of financial services

Every sector and industry needs a strong financial services industry. Businesses cannot grow unless they are supported by bank finance and families will not save or buy a house unless they believe the banks can be trusted. Without reform there remains a barrier to building a strong and fair economy.

We must not allow the reckless, greedy behaviour of a few in the banking sector to put taxpayers on the line for so much again, or to bring down the economy. That means effective and robust regulation. Under Labour there will be no return to business as usual for the banks after the recession.

Labour is leading the national and international debates on financial sector reform: on bank recapitalisation; the 50 per cent tax rate on bank bonus pots – likely to raise up to £3 billion this year; more powers for the Financial Services Authority to tackle excessive pay and improve supervision; cracking down on tax havens; and increasing liquidity and the capital that banks put aside so they cannot take such huge risks or pay excessive bonuses again. Labour is now leading the way on developing plans for an international insurance fee or transactions levy on derivatives and currency trading to curb excessive risk-taking.

While Labour is putting in place reforms to ensure a more responsible and better-regulated financial services sector, the Conservatives just do not get it. George Osborne welcomed a report from John Redwood MP calling for the deregulation of the mortgage sector just before it imploded. They also fail on judgement, opposing the nationalisation of banks including Northern Rock. So bad was George Osborne's judgement, even the *Financial Times* editorial felt compelled to write in September 2008:

If Mr Osborne had his way ... retail depositors would only be safe up to £50,000. Anything more would, as with all wholesale deposits, be unprotected. This would be foolhardy in today's perilous circumstances. It would be a big gamble with financial stability when confidence in banks is so low.

Under Labour, no retail depositor has lost their money. That would not have been the case if Labour had followed the advice of the Conservative Party. Without the action that Labour took we would have faced the total collapse of our financial sector. Osborne now tries to talk tough on the banks but the Conservatives opposed the 50 per cent bonus tax and only want a cap on bonuses for high street banks – not the investment banks, which played a big part in the crisis and where the largest bonuses are paid.

The Conservatives' answer to the crisis is to shut down the Financial Services Authority and give all its powers to the Bank of England. Having worked for most of my career at the Bank of England, I do not think this is a good idea. The Bank of England has a clear remit – to set interest rates to meet the inflation target. Adding in day-to-day regulation of all financial institutions will inevitably reduce the focus on inflation and interest rates which are so important for economic stability. The Bank, the Treasury and the FSA must improve their communication and the new Council for Financial Stability should help with that. But creating a giant institution that tries to do everything creates the risk of doing nothing very well.

We have an opportunity now to think radically about the financial sector we want. Labour is taking this opportunity while the Conservatives are happy to let the market decide with little concern for our collective interests.

One exciting idea, set out by Gordon Brown, is for a new, expanded role for the Post Office – providing financial services to local people. Unlike many banks the Post Office remains a trusted institution at the heart of our communities, giving it the opportunity to expand savings and financial services to more people.

Another idea is to turn Northern Rock and some other parts of the failed banks back into building societies – owned in common by their customers. We must re-think how financial services can best serve businesses, families and wealth creation, not just bankers.

Michael Stephenson
General Secretary, The Co-operative Party

One of the greatest lessons of the current economic crisis is that the values that drive our financial institutions are as important as the way they operate.

When they were in government the Tories encouraged our great building societies to demutualise. By legislating to change them from prudent, responsible mutual organisations to companies driven by short-term profit and greed they destroyed the mutual sector and cost taxpayers hundreds of millions of pounds.

Only Labour truly believes in having a strong mutual sector in our financial services industry. Voting Labour helps ensure we have an economy that is run for people, not just for profit.

Choices

The system we build in the wake of the financial crisis is up to us. Under Labour, financial markets will be structured on the premise that the banks cannot push the limits as far as they want; that self-interest does not automatically trump collective interest; and that the financial system is there to provide a service for customers, not a blank cheque for those in the boardroom. In place of the casino capitalism of the past, Labour will build a more principled capitalism.

Eddie Izzard, actor and comedian

The upcoming elections are going to have big consequences for people – for local schools, hospitals, police, for big issues right across society. I feel there is a clear choice – between a Labour government that would safeguard your future, and a Conservative one that would put it at risk. The Labour Party is the party of fairness, of public services, and of standing together when things are tough. So, I'll be using my vote for Labour – make sure you use yours too.

Markets must serve people, government action is needed to tackle the excesses of markets and international co-ordination is needed to secure the best deal here in the UK. These are Labour values and will define the Labour approach.

The Conservatives say: let markets decide and cut back the state. They say that we have to cut spending now and claim that there is no choice. But there is. Their choice is an age of austerity for people on modest and middle incomes – with cuts to services and support, while those on the highest incomes are not asked to contribute more but get a cut in inheritance tax instead. Labour's choice is a different one – a growth strategy to build the jobs of the future and a new age of aspiration and fairness, paying down the debt in a responsible way and tackling excessive risk-taking in the city. It is a fundamental choice on what sort of country you want Britain to be.

Working for an opportunity economy

I joined the Labour Party not long after the miners' strike, which was an intensely politicising experience for me. I remember crying with rage at what I saw on the television – police with batons charging working communities, who were standing up for their community way of life and for their work. It was this rage at profound injustice in the early 1980s that motivated me to, I think, actually lie about my age in order to join the Labour Party as soon as I could. I remember borrowing the money off my Dad.

RT HON. LIAM BYRNE MP

Extending opportunities

As we build the jobs of the future, we must ensure that everybody has the right to work matched with the responsibility to work if they can. Through the recession, Labour has matched its ambition with action to limit the increase in unemployment, and, as David Blanchflower highlighted in the last chapter, that has meant 500,000 fewer people out of work than most people predicted.

As well as helping create the jobs of the future, we must also ensure that work pays, that people can access jobs, that we are protected at work and that we have decent jobs with the chance to get on. These ambitions are at the heart of Labour's opportunity economy.

The effects of unemployment are scarring – to the individual and to society, while work offers a route out of poverty and opens up opportunities and possibilities.

There are still too many people who do not have a fair chance because the odds are stacked against them. The person desperate to work for whom a suitable job is not available; the mum who wants to work but cannot make it add up because of childcare; or the disabled person who would love to work but is held back because employers think they will be too much hassle. We have a responsibility to ensure that the right to work is a right for everyone.

Support through the recession – two approaches

In 1997 the UK did not have a welfare-to-work system, it had a system that abandoned people to a life on welfare. We had a Conservative government which had allowed unemployment to rise to over three million on two separate occasions. The Conservative Party believed unemployment was simply a result of market forces – little point of government intervention – all that was needed to stimulate employment was cuts in wages and social benefits. This attitude was summed up by Norman Lamont, who at the height of the 1991 recession, said that unemployment was a 'price well worth paying'.

The Conservative approach left the country with a legacy of worklessness and poverty, costing billions of pounds. That legacy had a very human face too – countless people denied the opportunities they deserved. By 1997, there were over two million more people on incapacity benefits than in 1979. The result of high unemployment and poverty wages was 3.4 million children living in poverty – a doubling in twenty years.

To hide growing unemployment the Conservatives moved people onto incapacity benefit so they did not appear in the jobless total. A generation of young people were written out of the picture, left to suffer the consequences.

Compare this to Labour's approach. When unemployment started to rise in 2008 Labour stepped up the support provided to people. Jobcentre Plus was expanded to support the rising number of claimants, new programmes such as the Young Person's Guarantee and the Future Jobs Fund were introduced and funding for people to gain new skills helped reduce the time taken to get back to work. By taking this proactive role, the government has stopped unemployment rising to three million, which had been predicted by nearly every economist.

Failing to support jobseekers to get back to work during the recession of the 1980s is thought to have allowed unemployment to rise by 4 percentage points more than it need have done. Labour did not abandon people during this downturn; we did more for them.

Even in tough times, we must hold true to our values of fairness, opportunity and social justice.

Towards full employment

Labour believes families and communities are better off with work – that is why Labour has always been committed to the goal of full employment. To tackle the legacy of unemployment and inactivity, Labour's priority in 1997 was to support people back to work and make work pay.

Over the past thirteen years, Labour has put in place more support than ever for people to enter work. With programmes for young people, the long-term unemployed and people on health-related benefits, you can now get the personalised support needed to find sustainable employment. Conservative neglect in the past meant high, demoralising youth unemployment. That is why in 1997 Labour introduced a one-off windfall tax on the privatised utilities to pay for the welfare-to-work scheme that helped more than two million young people back to work.

More childcare and guaranteed nursery places are opening up opportunities to families to balance work and family commitments better than they ever could have done before.

Nicci, Middlesex

Labour's childcare vouchers have helped my husband and me reach a great work–life balance. They have enabled us to employ a nanny for the two days a week I work in the office, and my husband has now gone down to four days a week, with me working that extra day – so we are with the children (aged six and one) for roughly an equal amount of time. Since we started using vouchers our childcare has been much more affordable – it means we can work a few extra hours here and there. I think childcare vouchers are fantastic for supporting parents who want to work, and we have got our childcare and work balance right for us and our children.

Prior to the financial crisis, the number of people on unemployment benefit was at its lowest level in thirty years with 3.1 million more people in work than in 1997. And while there is still a long way to go, Labour has ended the ongoing increase in the number of people claiming incapacity benefit, with the number of claimants actually falling since 2006. Even today, there are more than two million more people in work than in 1997.

At the same time as putting in place new programmes to help the unemployed, Labour has strengthened the requirements on people to look for work. Gone is the Conservative approach of allowing people to claim benefits without providing the support needed to get back to work. Labour believes that with the obligation on government to act, there is a reciprocal obligation on people to look for and find suitable employment. Indeed maintaining support for those who really need it requires taking action to ensure that the system is not abused.

Making work pay

The world of work in 2010 looks very different from 1997. Most obviously there is the National Minimum Wage, lifting thousands of people – often low paid women – out of poverty. The National Minimum Wage is one of the Labour achievements I am most proud of, enshrining the values of fairness and decency.

But things did not stop with its introduction. The National Minimum Wage has gone up each year, rising from £3.60 an hour when it was introduced to £5.80 in October 2009. This is equivalent to almost a £4,500 increase in the annual salary of a person working forty hours a week. The Conservatives said it would cost a million jobs, but instead it led to more people getting jobs and more families lifted out of poverty. Over one million workers benefit every year from the National Minimum Wage.

Such has been its success that the Conservatives have been forced to endorse it. Yet within the Conservative Party there remain people actively seeking to remove it. A bill introduced by Conservative MP Christopher Chope just last year, signed by eleven of his colleagues, sought to water down the minimum wage, allowing workers and employers to 'negotiate' lower pay, without a hint of concern about exploitation of the lowest-paid people.

Not only has Labour ensured that the rate has increased, but the minimum wage has been extended to 16–18-year-olds. And when Labour realised, following a trade union campaign, that restaurant owners were using a loophole in the legislation to make tips count towards a worker's National Minimum Wage rate, the government took action to close that loophole.

Even in the current economic situation, Labour has committed to increase the minimum wage year on year. If the Conservatives got to power would they abolish the minimum wage? More likely they would simply fail to increase it, so inflation would render it worthless. They would let the market decide wages, and poverty.

David, Sunderland

When Labour introduced the minimum wage I knew I had a chance to earn a decent wage for a decent day's work, unlike the Tory years where hard-working people could be paid peanuts.

Although the Tories have reluctantly agreed to keep the minimum wage what they haven't announced is whether they would increase it. How would they like to be stuck on £5.80 an hour for the next five years?

I know that I will be better off with Labour.

The Low Pay Commission, which recommends the rate at which the minimum wage is paid, has done excellent work in the last decade. But a fourth-term Labour government might usefully extend the work of the Commission to look at the causes of low pay and to improve the skills and opportunities available to low-paid workers to further tackle poverty. Reviewing and simplifying the benefits system – and ensuring that it always supports people back to work – should also be a priority for Labour's fourth term.

Fairness at work

Labour knows that what matters is not just a job, but good quality jobs – with good prospects, fair pay, protection from discrimination, autonomy, respect and the flexibility to combine work with other responsibilities – particularly family commitments.

Anna, Knottingley

I was able to take twenty-six weeks of maternity leave when I had my baby in August. I've also got a little boy of three, and I found it really hard to go back to work eighteen weeks after he was born – it was a real wrench. It was a lot easier this time as

I'd had longer with my baby. My husband also took paternity
leave, which was great – you need help after you've had a baby –
especially when you have other children as well.

When I went back to work, my employer accepted my
request to work fewer hours and let me work the days and
hours that I could.

Rights at work and fairness for working people are at the heart
of the Labour Party's vision and values. From the years before the
First World War, when economic turbulence led some employers to
pay near-starvation wages, to the Shaw Inquiry, when Ernie Bevin
was able to get dockers' wages raised, to the campaign for equal pay
for women and the introduction of the National Minimum Wage,
working conditions are central to Labour's existence.

Tony Woodley, Unite joint general secretary

The Labour Party was created by working people and trade
unions because it became clear that a political voice was
needed. The reasons people should support Labour today
remain the same. Labour remains the only party that is capable
of bringing about the sort of change that will improve the lives of
working people.

That is not to say the past thirteen years have been perfect
and there remains a great deal to be done. However, changes
in the law which mean employers have to recognise trade
unions if more than 50 per cent of the workforce want them,
greater protection for those taking industrial action, the right to
flexible working and to maternity and paternity pay are all big
achievements.

Under Labour, working people have new rights, including the

right to four weeks' paid holiday each year. For the first time ever, people no longer have to worry about taking holiday to spend time with their families for fear they could not afford to. The government has also set out plans to implement the Temporary and Agency Workers Directive, to ensure that bad employers cannot get round the law by employing temporary workers and denying them their rights.

A good job also means a safe job. This must be backed up by regulation – not red tape – but fair and decent health and safety requirements to protect working people. The government has introduced corporate manslaughter legislation, so that the boards of firms are now responsible for health and safety at work – especially important in the construction industry.

I have seen in Armley, at the heart of industrial Leeds, how badly things can go wrong when workers, and whole communities, are not protected from businesses who seek to exploit them, and how government can help to put right the excesses of markets.

If you talk to people in Leeds who lived near the old asbestos factory in Armley they will recount stories of the streets being thick with white asbestos dust – so thick that the children would make 'snowballs' out of it and throw them at one another, not realising that the same asbestos would come to blight their communities for generations. Local people did not know how dangerous asbestos could be but the evidence was there – and the factory owners ignored it. The local community paid the price. Similar stories are told up and down the country, particularly in working-class industrial areas. So, in 1999, the Labour government banned the use of all forms of asbestos in new buildings.

But for years, those with asbestos-related diseases were not able to sue the negligent employers if they became ill. So, in 2006, when the Law Lords made a decision which made it difficult for victims of fatal asbestos-related diseases to claim compensation, the Labour government took swift action to reverse that decision, enabling victims and their families to get the compensation they deserved.

We all have responsibilities to look for work, but business and government have responsibilities as well to ensure that we are protected when we go to work. Labour has done just that.

Joan Armatrading, musician

Under Labour, women's rights have got top billing:

- It was the Labour Party and Gordon Brown, against opposition, who pushed for the minimum wage and now the minimum wage helps a million people a year (two thirds of them women).
- It was the Labour government who introduced the winter heating allowance.
- People used to think you couldn't do much to stop violence against women. But there's been a 64 per cent decrease in incidents of domestic violence since 1997, the reporting of rape has doubled and the number of convictions has increased by around 50 per cent.
- Labour has also more than doubled the level of maternity pay and introduced the first ever system of paternity and adoption leave – again all of these were opposed.

In 2001 I completed my BA (Hons) degree through the Open University – a degree I combined with my schedule of recording and touring (I took my final exam the day after my last gig of the year!). It was the Labour Party that made it possible for anyone, at any point in their life, to enjoy higher education and to gain new skills.

I have spent enough of my life campaigning for equality to know real progress when I see it. Labour can keep us

---

moving forward, and that's why I think it's important to vote for continued progression under Labour.

Welfare reform

The recession revealed the inequality in people's resilience when times get tough. But these inequalities persist when the economy is growing too. As we build the future economy, we must expand opportunities – especially to those who have had fewer in the past – so that everyone has the chance to shape their own lives.

We must complete the transformation of the welfare state so that it can truly change people's lives – ensuring that support is tailored to people's individual needs and circumstances. Labour's welfare reforms match high expectations with high levels of support and have created an ambitious welfare policy with more emphasis on removing the barriers to work. Labour's vision is a system that, because it is more supportive and demanding, is more effective in enabling people to improve their lives.

The opportunity economy should provide opportunities to all – including those whose circumstances make it harder to take advantage of what work, and life, has to offer.

While everyone claiming jobseekers allowance is given proactive help in finding work, currently far fewer of those in receipt of so-called 'inactive benefits' – principally the disabled, lone parents and partners of benefit claimants – access support. As a result significant numbers spend long periods on benefits, all the while losing touch with the world of work and increasing their risk of poverty, social exclusion and poor health.

It is incumbent on government to help lift families, and children, out of poverty. Welfare reform can make a major contribution to meeting that goal. If we fail to act we will be denying opportunities to people who, more than most, need a fresh start. A mother who cannot read and write, but wants to support her children and demonstrate to them the value of hard work and self-reliance. The disabled person who needs extra help getting to work and getting around the office – but who is quite capable of working hard and doing a good job. Or the person who has struggled to hold down a job because of problems with drink and drugs, but who is now ready to work again, if only he could get the training and the confidence to get a job. These are the people welfare reform can support.

All the evidence confirms what is obvious to most people: the longer people are out of touch with work, the harder it is for them to get back there. While the specific steps taken or support accessed should be personalised, everyone who can participate should do so. In cases in which people choose not to engage, this could lead to a reduction in benefits.

This principle of work for those who can applies to Labour's plans for expecting those who have been claiming Jobseekers Allowance for two years to take part in full-time activity. This would involve intensive support, combining job-searching with work experience, to build people's skills so that they are not so remote from the world of work that getting a job becomes impossible. This would not be an easy ride and is not meant to be; it would remove the option for people to claim benefits while working 'on the side'.

None of this means forcing parents with young children back to work. But as your children get older you should be preparing to get back to work, balancing caring and work responsibilities as the majority of families do now. Labour has significantly increased parental leave and child benefit while the Working Tax Credit and the right to request flexible working help many parents combine working and caring. Nor does welfare reform mean people with serious disabilities having to work – on the contrary. Reform of the system will mean support for those who need it and more public support for a fairer system of welfare and work. A progressive welfare system asks more of citizens and requires more of government, but it is central to shaping a fairer society.

Lucinda, Leeds

I was born with a disability and for most of my career I have supported people with learning disabilities to live fulfilling lives and to access employment where possible. Labour has made a big difference in making education – at schools, colleges and universities – more accessible to people with disabilities, and now is helping people with disabilities to enter the job market. People with disabilities make a valuable contribution, and the Labour government recognises that for some people there remain barriers preventing them entering employment – and is beginning to break them down. The current employment rate for people with disabilities is around half; however, this is dramatically lower for a person with a learning disability at 7.5 per cent. I believe the Labour government is working towards a society where every person with a disability should be valued.

There are some people who will claim that increasing the mutual obligation on people to look for work is the wrong thing to do and a reactionary policy. However, in my own constituency, I know that families who play by the rules and go out to work every day are angry at the small minority of people who seem content to survive on benefits. Everyone should contribute to society, and when people do not play by the rules – whether it is the investment banker hiding his money in a tax haven or the person on benefits who could get a job – it is right that the government demands action. It is also clear that it is better for the individual to be in work – all the evidence shows that people in work are happier, better off and healthier than those on benefits. It is better for children too, especially as having parents in work makes it more likely that you will be lifted out of poverty and in time get a job too.

No one should be punished or stigmatised for receiving benefits, and society should support those who are caring full time or have the most serious disabilities. But in return for support, people must take responsibility for making the most of the opportunities they have.

Quality of work

Labour knows that the quality of our work and whether we enjoy being at work matters too. People are more likely to stay and succeed at work if they enjoy it and if feel they are treated fairly and have the opportunities to progress. Our quality of life is higher too when we are happy at work.

In the last decade, millions of people have been given a second chance to improve their basic literacy and numeracy at work and gain the qualifications they need to enter and progress in employment.

Linda, Liverpool

I was working as a part-time sales assistant when I got the chance to do some courses through my union learning rep.

I didn't like school and I didn't get many qualifications, so I was a bit nervous. But with some encouragement I did the government-funded basic skills courses in maths and English and really enjoyed them.

I then went on to do an introductory computer course. I had applied for promotion some years ago and not been accepted so I thought I was stuck in the job I had. Passing my courses gave me the self-confidence to apply again and I was delighted when I got the job as assistant manager. Now I've been promoted again to store manager of a larger store.

I am really happy in my work now – I feel that I'm using my

skills and experience. I'm obviously better off financially as well and that's great. I still want to carry on learning and I'll be doing a more advanced computer course next.

Labour believes in giving people the opportunity to progress, learn new skills and reach their full potential. With a changing labour market where the concept of a 'job for life' is fast disappearing, we need to keep pace with these changes. The alternative, Conservative, approach is summed up by David Willetts, the Conservative Shadow Secretary of State for Skills, who said: 'There is no evidence whatsoever that getting better educated or better trained is a way of helping unemployed people into work.' He went on to say that it was a myth that pouring 'more investment in education and training into the empty vessels of these unemployed people' would have an impact.

The Conservative approach is at odds with the reality of modern Britain. Most people know someone who has the prospect of losing their job. We know that to find a job sometimes means learning new skills. This is not about pouring money into 'empty vessels', it is about providing people with a helping hand to succeed – to fulfil ambitions and aspirations and succeed in the opportunity economy.

High quality jobs mean achieving a work–life balance, representation in the workplace, having employers and managers we trust, and a stake in the organisations we work for. Decent jobs can improve our self-esteem and health and enable us to achieve our ambitions.

Realising our ambitions

Labour's vision is for a strong and stable economy, where the responsibility of an individual to get a job and training is matched with the businesses responsibility to train their workforce, pay them a fair wage, treat them with respect and dignity, and help them meet their work and home commitments.

These responsibilities must be met with a corresponding role for government in making work pay with a minimum wage and tax credits to support people in work.

We must ensure that the welfare state backs up these aspirations – enabling people rather than maintaining the status quo. A proactive welfare state can ensure that more people are in work and fewer in poverty; where people are in control of their lives, balancing work commitments and family responsibilities. Then we will build a fairer and more equal society where opportunities to fulfil your dreams are available to all. A strong and stable economy cannot be achieved by the market alone – it requires a supportive government too.

We have the opportunity to emerge from the recession more confident and radical in shaping a fairer and more equal society, where everyone has the power and capabilities to live the life they seek. Labour's approach to work, skills and welfare reform can ensure that this is the economy we build together.

The case for climate action

I joined the Labour Party because I believe that it will put the needs of the poorest first and I hope to see it maintain power in 2010. I particularly want to see the continued investment in overseas development and tackling the big issues of the day including climate change, unfair international trade, unfair tax systems and third world debt.

PAUL, WITNEY

The challenge that confronts us

Tackling climate change is one of the biggest challenges that we face. It is a challenge that involves each and every one of us, not just world leaders, and it is our generation that will be judged on how we respond. It is the values of the Labour Party – on the need for international co-operation; government, not just market solutions; and the importance of a socially just response – that mean Labour is best able to deal with the challenges of climate change.

Last year I visited Svalbard, in the Norwegian Arctic Circle. I met with the Polar Institute, among others, to learn first-hand about the impact of climate change on this fragile region. Beyond the common image of the polar bear or the husky, the scars of human activity are readily seen – be it the slag heaps and concentrations of the coal industry, the melting of the ice cap or the increasingly volatile nature of the seasons.

In recent decades the Arctic has been heating twice as fast as the rest of the world. Without concerted action to reduce the world's greenhouse gas emissions, between 1990 and 2100 the Arctic temperatures are projected to rise by 6 to 7 degrees. The rate at which the ocean is warming is dramatically changing the environment. Perhaps most vividly, the melting ice means that by as soon as 2013, ships will likely be able to sail straight across the North Pole for at least part of the year, meaning shorter and more lucrative shipping routes from China and Russia to the West. If these routes are developed it will further damage the environment, and would represent a stark failure of the international community to tackle climate change.

But you do not have to go to Norway to see what climate change is doing. In November last year floods more than 12 feet above the normal river level in some places engulfed Cockermouth in Cumbria, and in 2007 there were severe floods across the UK. Climate change means extreme weather events will become more likely. We will have hotter summers and wetter winters, and without concerted action, the heatwave in Europe in 2003, which caused 35,000 extra deaths, will be the norm by the 2040s.

We are the first generation tasked with tackling climate change, and, while it will outlast us, the actions we take now will have a profound effect on every generation after us.

The evidence

The scientific evidence is robust: to avoid the most dangerous effects of climate change we must limit the global temperature rise to 2 degrees Celsius. Above this global changes are simply unmanageable: up to 30 per cent of known species would be at an increased risk of extinction; the world's malarial zones would increase by over 25 per cent; and more than 150 million people could become environmental refugees.

The UN Intergovernmental Panel on Climate Change concluded that recent climate change is largely caused by human activity, and that without determined action global temperatures could rise by between 1.8 and 4 degrees Celsius by the end of the century above the levels of the 1980s and 1990s. In their worst-case predictions, they could soar by 6.4 degrees. All of these scenarios would have a dramatic impact, including unpredictable weather conditions, food shortages and a huge displacement of people.

We have a moral responsibility to protect the earth and its resources. We have stewardship of this planet for the generations that follow us; we do not have the right to squander the world's resources without consideration for our children, or their children.

While the moral case is compelling, the Stern Review commissioned by Gordon Brown when he was Chancellor set out the economic costs of climate change. Without action, we face precipitous economic costs, of between 5 per cent and 20 per cent of global GDP. But while the costs of inaction are great, tackling climate change provides opportunities to build a stronger and more sustainable economy – set out in chapter one.

There is a broad consensus on the evidence, and government, business and individuals are acting. However, there are Conservative MPs who will not believe the scientific evidence, with former Conservative Cabinet Minister, and advisor to David Cameron on deregulation, John Redwood MP writing about the 'global warming swindle'. The next generation of Conservatives seem to agree with John Redwood: in a recent survey of 140 Conservative parliamentary candidates, climate change ranked as nineteenth out of nineteen in terms of their priorities. A potential Prime Minister needs to lead his party and carry people with him to deliver change – it is not clear that David Cameron is able to do that.

What has already been done?

With Labour, UK policy and priorities recognise the increasing urgency of climate change. Britain's leadership was most apparent in Copenhagen where Gordon Brown was the first head of government to commit to attending the summit, arriving early to help hammer out a deal.

The most important achievement at Copenhagen was a 2 degrees Celsius warming target, based on the scientific evidence. This agreement is down to the efforts of world leaders, and particularly Gordon Brown and Ed Miliband, Secretary of State for Energy and Climate Change, who argued consistently for this baseline.

In addition, immediate finance was agreed to help developing countries deal with the effects of climate change. Building on this, Gordon Brown's proposal for a $100 billion annual fund by 2020 was agreed by countries including the United States on the penultimate day of the summit. This is a big step forward, and will help developing countries adapt to climate change and support access to new technologies to help bypass the energy-intensive stage of production that Britain – and the developed world – went through during the Industrial Revolution. If we can support this transition, then the economic growth needed to lift people out of poverty will be possible without choking the planet.

Significant progress was made, but not as much as Britain wanted. The disappointment of Copenhagen is that the Accord isn't legally binding and didn't commit countries to specific cuts in emissions. It is essential that all countries now set the ambitious targets required, and then meet them. Our efforts must continue.

Despite no global deal, Europe is leading the way with a commitment to reducing its overall energy emissions to at least 20 per cent below 1990 levels by 2020. Britain is ambitious for Europe to raise its aspirations further and is ready to scale up this reduction to as much as 30 per cent under a new global climate change agreement when other developed countries make comparable efforts.

David Taylor works for an environmental NGO

This Labour government must take huge credit for the leadership it has shown in tackling climate change in the UK and internationally. Just as with the Make Poverty History campaign in 2005, Britain's leadership has been the result of a constructive relationship between a Labour government showing leadership and noisy civil society pushing for action.

The UK Climate Change Act is historic and a world first, binding us by law to reducing our emissions. Britain's Low Carbon Transition Plan lays out how we are going to achieve a low carbon economy, create millions of new jobs, tackle fuel poverty, and achieve a better standard of living in the process.

On the international stage, Gordon Brown and Ed Miliband have shown great personal leadership. The PM was the first world leader to go to Copenhagen and put billions of aid on the table up front to help developing countries adapt to climate change – and crucially made the commitment that 90 per cent of this would be additional to our existing aid budget. Ed Miliband, meanwhile, worked for days without sleep and arguably made a crucial last-minute intervention that stopped the talks from complete collapse.

I'm proud of what our government has done in the UK and on the international stage to lead on tackling climate change in a way that puts the needs of the poorest first, both in our society and around the globe.

What needs to be done to tackle climate change?

As world leaders continue to negotiate, there are five key areas where action needs to be taken – on targets, financing, technology, deforestation and adaptation.

First, on targets, both developed and developing countries have a role to play. Now that countries across the world are in the process of agreeing to reductions in their emissions for the first time, these must be made legally enforceable as soon as possible. But, even before a treaty, countries must act and a form of transparency needs to be developed so countries can stand by their commitments while retaining national sovereignty.

While UN processes need to adapt, it is imperative that it is the UN that takes the lead. The UN represents every nation on earth, and climate change depends on the actions of, and affects, every nation on earth. The UN embodies legitimacy that no other institution can confer.

Second, on financing it is crucial that we support the developing world to move to a low carbon growth model. Developed nations must make the proposed $100 billion annual fund – of public and private money – a reality by 2020.

Third, climate change presents us with the opportunity to develop new technologies that will limit the need for non-renewable energy sources. If the world has a lot to fear from climate change, it has even more to gain from new industries and clean technologies, with the potential to create hundreds of thousands of new and high-skill jobs. We must harness the ideas and the creativity of scientists and engineers – who have led the industrial and technological revolutions of the past – to meet these new challenges. Whether it is electric cars, carbon capture and storage or offshore wind, there is huge scope for a revolution in the way we produce and consume things.

It is for these reasons that Chancellor Alistair Darling has committed to a new funding mechanism to support carbon capture and storage demonstration projects, which if successful could lead the way towards using coal in environmentally sustainable ways both in the UK and abroad. By investing in new technologies, the UK can become a global leader in the low carbon industries that the world needs.

Britain also leads the world in offshore wind generation, and

Labour is committed to developing our capacity even further. Labour has set aside up to £170 million of funding to support a step change in investment, which could create up to 70,000 high-skilled jobs in Britain. Under Labour 15 per cent of all energy will be fuelled by renewable sources by 2015. Despite their 'vote blue, go green' slogan, research by Greenpeace shows that Conservative councils block more wind farms than they consent to, while the opposite is true of Labour councils. If you are serious about tackling climate change you have to back it up with resolute action.

Fourth, we must tackle deforestation if we are going to tackle climate change. Saving the rainforests was one of the earliest rallying calls of the environmental movement; it is also one of the most enduring. Deforestation remains a crucial problem – over 18 per cent of global emissions come from forestry. The UK wants to see an end to global forest loss by 2030 at the latest, and again, international agreement is needed.

Fifth, because climate change is already a reality to many in the developing world, funding to adapt to change is essential. Investment must be put into flood-resistant homes and using new crops that are more resilient to drought. The Labour government has funded projects in Bangladesh and Africa to do just that. As well as being the right thing to do, these projects are crucial in ensuring that conflicts over resources do not escalate as a result of climate change.

Adaptation means projects at a practical and local level, both in the UK and internationally. I recently met a co-operative of local people who want to build a sustainable housing project in West Yorkshire. Their mission is for affordable, environmentally sustainable housing, and to 'build a beautiful, safe neighbourhood where people come first and have direct power over how their neighbourhood is run'. Responding to climate change means doing things differently, but this could enhance our lives as well as making them more sustainable for our generation and the next.

Why Labour is the party to deal with climate change

In Britain and across the world, it is the progressive left, including the Labour Party in the UK, which has been leading the debate and can deliver the relief from climate change that we need.

Labour knows that tackling climate change requires a strategic role for government, stronger regulation of markets, an international strategy, and with social justice at its core.

The challenge of climate change requires a strategic role for government because without government action our targets for reductions in emissions simply will not be met or enforced.

To make the difference, government needs to work with others, including consumer groups, energy suppliers, supermarkets and local government. Working together we can make a green lifestyle simpler and more affordable. Practical steps like insulating our walls, lagging our lofts, recycling, using the bus rather than our car or even putting a solar panel on our roofs, all make a difference. Government must keep making it easier, and offer the incentives, for people to do the right thing.

This must include support to make our housing more energy efficient. Seventy per cent of the homes we will be living in by 2050 already exist, and the vast majority were built before any awareness of climate change, so we need to invest in improving the energy efficiency of the housing stock. A piecemeal market-only approach will not produce the action required. Labour has committed that up to seven million homes will have had an eco-makeover by 2020. Government is helping with the boiler scrappage scheme and subsidies for home insulation, as well as a commitment to building the zero carbon homes of the future.

The Warm Front scheme has already lifted over two million people out of fuel poverty – installing loft and cavity wall insulations to make our homes more energy efficient. Now the government is working with the business and voluntary sectors on an energy cashback scheme, providing free solar panels for social housing and more affordable electricity for people on low incomes – by connecting the panels to the National Grid. This will benefit 35,000 homes by 2011, reducing energy bills by an average of £150 a year.

Hugh Goulbourne, Huddersfield, SERA energy co-ordinator

This winter's big freeze has demonstrated exactly why the UK must continue to invest in energy-saving solutions.

Labour's policies have produced groundbreaking schemes. For example in Kirklees in West Yorkshire, local authorities, energy companies and building suppliers, working together, have gone house by house and street by street to help residents save energy and protect themselves from rising energy bills.

Labour's new Community Energy Savings Programme will ensure that energy companies spend around £350 million – in partnership with local authorities and community organisations – so that we can make sure that every home in the country becomes energy efficient.

Labour's recognition of the positive role of government contrasts starkly with the Conservatives' fundamental belief in a smaller state. In his last party conference speech before the general election, David Cameron chose to pursue this argument, arguing that smaller government was the solution.

Cameron's beliefs about the role of the state are inconsistent with the action required to tackle climate change. For change to happen efficiently and effectively government needs to take the lead, otherwise temperatures will continue to rise as we move too slowly and inconsistently towards our goals. To be successful we cannot afford to employ a strategy where the state sits on the sidelines, leaving action to the market alone. Under Labour, action has started but more will be needed in the years to come.

The effective tackling of climate change also requires the acceptance that markets need to be regulated. Left to their own devices, markets will continue to favour high-carbon transactions without recognising their cost to the environment. It is not enough to say that businesses should act responsibly; where they do not, regulation is required. Labour's philosophy is that government must provide sufficient regulation to combat market excesses that conspire against our common interests.

The last century has shown that in Britain it has always fallen to progressive forces to respond to the injustices and inequities that markets throw up. Now more than ever, we need effective regulation and incentives to ensure that businesses and individuals move towards lower-carbon modes of operation. The Labour government is committed to rewarding businesses and individuals who take measures to build our new green economy and the jobs that this can generate.

There is no high carbon, low cost future, so we must invest in renewable and sustainable forms of energy to ensure stable and affordable energy in the future. That is why Labour is investing in wind power, carbon capture and storage, renewable energy, and the roll-out of new smart electricity and gas meters, to help individuals track their energy usage and make informed decisions. Labour's aim is that every home in the country will have a smart meter by 2020.

Although we can take action at home, climate change is an inherently global challenge. Actions by one country – whether good or bad – have ramifications for us all. On each component of the approach to tackling climate change – targets, financing, technology, deforestation and adaptation – negotiating internationally is crucial.

Even if Britain stopped all of its carbon emissions today, China's growth would replace them within two years. It is clear that we must negotiate with other countries to have any chance in protecting ourselves, and the planet, against the impact of climate change.

At an international level, the EU is at the forefront of efforts to deal with climate change. For Britain, agreeing targets at an EU level has the big advantage of removing any competitive disadvantage from adapting our behaviour, as all countries in the EU must sign up – and of course, more than half of our trade is with other European countries. Through internationally co-ordinated actions, no country needs to sacrifice its own short-run economic growth but instead can commit to long-term measures that are economically and environmentally sustainable.

The first incarnation of what is now the EU, the European Coal and Steel Community, was formed in 1952 to promote peace and trade across Europe as it recovered from the Second World War. Today, the Foreign Secretary, David Miliband, has talked of 'a new EU – an Environmental Union' to meet the economic and resource challenges that confront us. This new EU could include an extension of the European Union's Emissions Trading Scheme, raising the carbon price and linking with emerging carbon markets to form a global trading scheme. While Labour is at the heart of Europe it can influence these international negotiations. By forming the European Conservatives and Reformists Group, the Conservatives have withdrawn themselves to the fringes of Europe. And, allying themselves with climate change sceptics, they have extinguished any negotiating power they may have had and along with it Britain's opportunity to influence the debate under a Conservative government.

Labour was elected in 1997 on a platform of economic prosperity and social justice. Like the challenges Labour has confronted in the past, not least in the creation of the welfare state, climate change is an economic and social justice challenge.

Labour is helping British families and pensioners on modest incomes, by increasing the grants that have already helped over two million people make their homes more energy efficient and cheaper to heat. The Labour government will ensure that the transition to a low carbon economy happens without undue financial stress for families on modest and middle incomes.

Samantha, North Wales

I have always believed that everyone has a responsibility to our planet – that all people should play their part in the fight against climate change and practise energy efficiency. I have installed energy-saving light bulbs in our house, and I try to unplug appliances when I'm done with them. A huge help in saving energy at home has been the government grant I received to have my loft and walls insulated. The work was done with minimum fuss and with 33 per cent of a home's heat lost through the walls, the insulation and draught-proofing work has helped me to conserve heat and reduce my heating bills each month. I also feel that I am playing my part in the fight against climate change.

Our responsibilities to fairness extend beyond our borders. Poorer countries are already suffering from climate change. In places such as Garissa in northern Kenya, families have been forced to leave their homes by flash floods. In Bangladesh, Cyclone Sidr took thousands of lives. The United Nations estimate that 90 per cent of disasters are now climate related.

A socially just response means minimising the damage that poor countries are exposed to, helping communities build more sustainable homes, and developing new crops and industries. The UK's Department for International Development is working in places like Bangladesh on projects helping communities to put their homes on stilts to prevent against flooding.

But while we know that we must make changes to the way we produce and consume, we must not falsely conclude that responding to climate change means zero growth, as some claim. The zero-growth approach plays to the worst fears of India, China, and many poorer countries, as they fear that developed countries are using climate change as an excuse to maintain the unequal status quo between developed and developing countries.

We need sustainable growth, with innovation driving green growth as entrepreneurs and business respond to new demands and pressures from consumers and government. We must ensure that poorer countries get access to technologies to ensure that they can grow sustainably too.

Tackling climate change means improving the lives of the poorest people in the world, but in ways that are more sustainable for all of us – and future generations too.

A more radical approach?

Labour will continue to take the tough decisions on climate action with an inspiring and practical fourth-term agenda, with plans for high-speed rail, low carbon vehicles and investment in electric cars, greener homes and offshore wind. The transition will require investment but will also mean more secure energy supplies, more energy-efficient homes, better-paid, higher-skilled jobs, cleaner cities and faster and better transport. This is a future where we all have a contribution to make and where we all have something to gain.

But there is more that could be done. In the transition to a low carbon economy, emissions trading and a higher carbon price potentially provide strong investment incentives – with government setting clear frameworks within which the private sector can take long-term commercial decisions. Businesses will be more confident about building wind farms or producing clean coal if it makes business sense to do so. The initial experience of the European Emissions Trading Scheme has been disappointing to date – with the price of carbon too low to really drive changes in behaviour. The need now is to look, quite urgently, at the options for ensuring we have a carbon price that is more stable and truly reflects its environmental costs.

New green ISAs and investment funds could help individuals to support the green economy of the future – with a role for government or an independent accreditation scheme for kite-marking such funds. Local authorities and communities have a role to play too, as pioneering schemes including solar panels in social and private housing and the energy efficiency makeovers piloted in some areas have shown. There is potential for community energy generation – connected to the National Grid, creating local solutions to the dual challenges of energy security and efficiency. There is also huge capacity for local authorities to act through introducing their own carbon budgets and targets for reducing energy consumption – as government departments have done.

Climate change requires actions from individuals, communities, central and local government and through international co-ordination.

Conclusion

The campaigner Margaret Mead once said: 'Never doubt that a small group of thoughtful, committed people can change the world. Indeed, it is the only thing that ever has.' That is undoubtedly true with climate change. Whether it was apartheid in South Africa, civil rights in America, votes for women, or the Jubilee 2000 or Make Poverty History campaigns, it has been civil society leading the change. The activists and global citizens who campaigned for urgent action at Copenhagen summit show that people have mobilised once more. What is needed now is a framework to co-ordinate the initiatives and actions being taken individually to ensure that the common good succeeds against short-run self-interest.

The Labour Party was founded to champion the aspirations and ideas of ordinary working families in a period where privilege and wealth were the only determinants of power. It is those enduring values of co-operation, fairness and social justice that will enable us to respond successfully to the challenges of climate change, whether it is tackling fuel poverty, investing in new industries, or providing help to people in the developing world.

Tackling climate change is our new 'great society' mission. An active government and international co-ordination, with businesses and citizens empowered to play their part, can make the change that we need. It is Labour that has the experience and values to inspire this new contract and in turn ensure that we get a global deal on climate change and hand to the next generation a viable, secure and sustainable planet.

Britain in the world

I joined the Labour Party because it has brought great change to the UK; it fights for fairness and opportunities for people from all walks of life. I believe that the future of the UK depends on having a strong Labour Party and government in order to progress further as a nation; we have come a long way since 1997 but have more to do.

GRAHAM, LONDON

Acting with common purpose

Britain's history can only be told with reference to its role in the world. Europe and the Commonwealth are integral to our island's story, and with the distinction between domestic and international fast breaking down, our future is undoubtedly global as well.

Economic trends, including more open global markets, and technological innovation, particularly in communications, have strengthened the connections between individuals, businesses, societies and economies. Travel is faster and cheaper than ever, while the flow of ideas and capital around the world is virtually instantaneous. These changes are positive, empowering and create opportunities for us all. But they also create new challenges.

Britain can only solve the challenges it faces by acting with common purpose with our allies and new coalitions. As more decisions require Britain to influence the global political debate, we need a British government with the authority and leadership to win support for our values and vision, and we must continue to face out to the world if we are to thrive in it. Under Gordon Brown's leadership Britain has played a pivotal international role, on climate change, the financial crisis and in confronting terrorism – helping secure our domestic objectives and meet our international obligations.

Alex Bigham, Foreign Policy Centre

Any attempt to divide 'over there' from 'over here' is rooted in the politics of the last century. No politics is local anymore. Dealing with the local environment on your doorstep is the responsibility of a councillor, but you can't divorce that issue from climate change. Gordon Brown's leadership on the world economic stage has had a real affect on jobs and lives where I live, in Lambeth.

Terrorism, climate change and financial chaos require global responses and collective action, and only true internationalists can do that. It can't be done by those who are threatened by or hostile to Europe. It can't be done by those sceptical of climate change.

Ten years ago, no-one would have predicted a decade which saw the election of the first black American President, the events of 9/11, or the worst recession since the Second World War. As Heraclitus put it, 'the only constant is change'. It is the response to new challenges that defines true international leadership. I believe in Labour's 'progressive patriotism' – using our values in multilateral action and international co-operation to achieve democracy, security and prosperity for all.

Across the world, it will be progressive parties like Labour who can best meet the demands of this new century: not only the challenges we know today, but more importantly the challenges we can't even imagine today.

The challenges facing Britain domestically and internationally increasingly overlap. One of the most important – climate change – has been discussed elsewhere in this book. This chapter focuses on

international security, global poverty and finding modern responses
to such shared challenges.

International security

Britain today faces a different range of security threats than in the
past. The use of suicide bombers, orchestrated by terrorist cells
often with no clear chain of command, presents dangers that are
hard to contain and predict. To defeat them we must respond on
a number of levels: with military, development, construction and
peacebuilding projects.

It is for our security that British troops are in Afghanistan. The
destruction and human tragedy wrought by al-Qaeda in London
and New York remain with us and serve as a constant reminder
as to why the work of British soldiers, alongside forces from over
forty other nations, is so vital. Failed states, such as Afghanistan, are
fertile breeding grounds for recruiting new enemy combatants and
if the power vacuum is not filled by a viable, democratic Afghani
government, supported by the global community, it will again be
filled by al-Qaeda.

By training the Afghanistan Army we are helping build the
legitimacy and effectiveness of international efforts to rid the region
of terrorism. Three years ago the Afghani Army had 60,000 troops.
By the end of this year, there will be 134,000 Afghani soldiers –
trained by British and NATO forces – defending their own country
and improving international security.

But we know that peace in Afghanistan will take more than
military action and training. Progress is also being made in building
the local infrastructure and a stronger civil society. Some 82 per
cent of the population now live in districts which have access to
basic healthcare, and women are playing a much greater role in
society. In Helmand province, where the majority of British forces
are in operation, eighty-one schools are now open, up from thirty-

four in 2006. Girls are going to school again, a freedom denied to them by the Taliban. Of the 165,000 teachers paid for by Britain's Department for International Development, 28 per cent are women. It is through working with and supporting local communities in Afghanistan that we will secure peace.

The price of achieving our objectives is high, especially for servicemen and women on the front line and for their families. Casualties in 2009 were the highest since those sustained in the Falklands War. British soldiers, working with our NATO and United Nations partners, have made a huge contribution to this fledgling democracy and to British security, and our armed forces are a credit to our country and deserve our utmost respect and recognition. British forces are fighting for security in Afghanistan and at home. We cannot, and Labour will not, turn our back on Afghanistan now. If we did, Afghanistan, and Pakistan, would become a crucible for violence and for terrorists who would seek to inflict casualties on a mass scale on our streets. We must work to ensure that we build a strong and sustainable police force, army and government so that the Afghani people can govern and defend themselves – free of corruption, terror and extremism.

While military operations continue in Afghanistan, in April of last year British combat operations in Iraq came to an end. We leave behind a democracy that will finally allow Iraqis to share in the natural wealth of their country. The tyranny and oppression of Saddam Hussein's regime, and the insecurity that followed his fall from power, have given way to a burgeoning civil society with much hope and promise. In Basra, where British forces were based, 70 per cent of people now benefit from a proper sewerage system, compared to less than a quarter in 2003, while around one million people have benefited from investment in electricity supply. With our support, 2½ million people across Iraq have access to safe drinking water, over 1,000 schools have been re-built and over

4.7 million schoolchildren have been provided with textbooks and materials. The operations of British troops have helped create the framework in which stability and security can flourish.

But this legacy should not obscure the difficulties and setbacks of the past seven years. An honest appraisal must confront the problems faced and areas where we could have done better. Not least, we must understand the lack of post-conflict preparation, and how intelligence failures were allowed to incorrectly conclude that Saddam Hussein possessed weapons of mass destruction. This is why Sir John Chilcot was asked by Gordon Brown to conduct his extensive inquiry to help us learn the lessons of the conflict.

While international terrorist organisations and failed states pose a new threat to Britain, nuclear weapons and nuclear proliferation continue to destabilise the international community. The number of nuclear weapons has fallen since the end of the Cold War – but such achievements risk being undermined by Iran. A nuclear Iran would throw the Middle East into a new arms race and jeopardise hopes for peace in that region. That is why Britain is working with the UN and the International Atomic Energy Agency to contain Iran's nuclear threat and build stability in the region.

Active engagement in the Middle East, pursuing a two-state solution for Israel and Palestine, is a key priority. Sustained efforts have been made by Foreign Secretaries from Robin Cook to David Miliband, pushing diplomatic measures to bring the parties together and funding humanitarian projects that are making a difference in Palestine.

I saw first hand on a recent trip to the Middle East the effects of active intervention from the Labour government, from support for the Palestinian private sector to developing a modern professional police force in the West Bank. Labour is committed to strong relationships with Israel and the Palestinian Authority, encouraging Israel to continue to improve freedom of movement for Palestinians and cease West Bank construction; calling for an end to Palestinian rocket and mortar attacks against the people of southern Israel; and encouraging Palestinian leaders to return to the negotiating table in order to agree the final borders of a viable, contiguous, Palestinian state alongside a safe and secure Israel. Our domestic security is irrevocably tied to international security in a world ever more inter-connected.

International development

Our responsibility to the developing world first and foremost is a moral imperative. The fairness that drives our policy at home extends to a belief that it is wrong for somebody's life chances to depend on where they are born in the world. And in a world where the challenges of conflict and insecurity, climate change and disease have global effects, it is also the right, practical course to take.

That global poverty is now so high on political agendas is in large part due to pressure from coalitions of decent and compassionate people. By the turn of the century, debt relief and international development had, under Tony Blair's and Gordon Brown's leadership, become political priorities. In 2005, when the G8 met in Gleneagles, it became an international priority too.

The response of the British public – whether to the Haitian earthquake, scenes of hunger in sub-Saharan Africa, or by the millions of people who wore a white band in 2005, shows people's generosity, and the successes of world-leading UK charities like Oxfam and Save the Children. But the voluntary sector knows, and Labour knows, that you cannot tackle global poverty by charity alone. We need to co-ordinate action, because sustainable solutions require global political will and collective, multilateral action and commitments. The UK is engaged at the heart of this movement, be it in spearheading reforms of the United Nations, World Bank and European Union or in securing global support for financing the fight against climate change.

Bono, musician

I like Gordon Brown. He's a serious man for serious times, and many people aren't aware of his achievements, from when he was Chancellor to Prime Minister now.

In the last ten years there have been thirty-four million extra children going to school in Africa, 3.2 million extra people on AIDS drugs or anti-viral drugs, and half the amount of deaths from malaria. These are extraordinary statistics, and the Prime Minister deserves the credit because he was part of it. I'm sure it goes right to the core of the Labour Party.

An accident in geography should not decide whether you live or die. To have AIDS in London or Birmingham is not a death sentence, and it's not acceptable that it's a death sentence in Africa.

The recession has hit Britain hard, but it has hit people in the developing world a lot harder. We need to stand firm with our commitments to the Millennium Development goals. Britain and the Prime Minister have stuck to their promises in good and bad times, moving the concepts of equality and justice for people in the developing world. This is a monumental achievement and I don't know if the people of Britain know what they have pulled off.

This is what makes Britain great!

In stark contrast to the Conservative years, the Labour government has invested in international development – as campaigners and charities recognise.

Jo Cox, director of a development charity

It's hard to recall the UK's record on development before 1997, but here are a few reminders: a dwindling aid budget repeatedly cut, tied aid, an area of government so marginalised it didn't even have its own Cabinet Minister.

Over the past decade I've had a front row seat in the life-saving revolution that Labour has led to tackle global poverty. Working for Oxfam, and with many other charities, I've seen first hand how Labour's policies and leadership have achieved numerous historic breakthroughs: on debt relief, which let millions more kids go to school; on health, which will allow millions more pregnant women and their children to access the care they need; and becoming the first country in the world to offer a legislative guarantee that it will honour its promises on aid.

But it's not just good policies that count, it's the passion and commitment which underpins them which allowed Labour to turn our country into the global gold standard in fighting poverty. British people are incredibly generous, twenty-five years after Live Aid and five after Live8, it's important that we have a government that cares as much about justice as we do.

Setting up the first Department for International Development in 1997, Labour ended the disgraceful era of development aid being given only in exchange for trade deals. No longer was aid about helping ourselves, more than helping those in desperate need. In the years since, the aid budget has been tripled and been made more effective.

It is wrong for a child to die for want of clean water, or from an easily preventable disease, or be deprived of basic learning because of a lack of money. So, in the last year alone we have delivered seven million anti-malarial bed-nets, saving around 80,000 lives. Around the world we have vaccinated three million children against measles, preventing 30,000 deaths, and provided life-saving drugs to almost 100,000 people living with HIV/Aids. The support given by Labour has been targeted at the poorest, encouraging growth, good governance, development and international engagement. It has got water, health and education to people who need basic public services the most. The Millennium Development Goals to tackle world poverty by 2015, agreed at Gleneagles, are a powerful symbol of collective action, building on the action taken in the UK.

I am proud that the Labour government is the first government in history to commit to a law that 0.7 per cent of GDP must be given in foreign aid. Our domestic challenges will not detract from the war on global poverty. If we fail to achieve the Millennium Development Goals we will not only have failed in our moral duty, but we will have shown political and economic short-sightedness. Globalisation has made us all neighbours. Migration caused by economic hardship, civil unrest or climate change will have a direct impact on our cities and towns. Preachers of hate find easier converts where no opportunities exist. This makes international development a practical imperative as well as a moral quest.

Labour's multilateral, moral and progressive approach stands in stark contrast to the shallow detoxification strategy that motivates the Conservatives.

Although David Cameron has endorsed Labour's achievements, in a recent poll of Conservative parliamentaray candidates, 90 per cent saw no reason to make the protection of the aid budget a priority while Conservative grandees such as Douglas Hurd have called for the Department for International Development to be abolished.

The ideology that drives many in the Conservative Party would see the achievements of the last thirteen years reversed. In a time of economic difficulty, the people most in need would be left to fend for themselves. Theirs is an outdated approach, which believes at best that markets and individual generosity alone can deliver the change needed, and at worst that it is not our responsibility to find the systematic solutions that would end the root causes of poverty. Ultimately their record speaks for itself. Under the Conservatives, aid halved. Under Labour since 1997, it has trebled.

It is a moral duty to actively tackle poverty, and it makes practical sense to pursue this moral imperative as a matter of priority.

Modern responses

To find the answers we need to the challenges and opportunities we face means working in partnership with our allies, new coalitions and international institutions. Gordon Brown has been at the forefront of forging a global financial and economic response which prevented the complete collapse of the banking system and the chaos that would have ensued. It was also Gordon Brown's leadership which developed the G20's $1.1 trillion recovery plan to bring the world out of recession.

As the global economy recovers from the crisis, it is essential that we tackle its underlying causes and put in place better mechanisms for co-operation on our long-term economic objectives. We know that markets alone will not deliver outcomes that are in our collective interests. It is also true that countries pursuing economic policies in isolation will not deliver the best outcome for themselves or the world economy. So, because one cause of the crisis was unco-ordinated economic policies – with too much spending in the West and too much saving in the East – the UK secured agreement at the G20 for a new global economic growth strategy and co-operation.

Gordon Brown has also led the debate on ways to ensure the financial sector pays for the cost of government interventions to repair the banking system and protects taxpayers in the future. The ideas being discussed include an international levy on banks that, because of their size or business, may represent a source of risk to the financial system. Gordon Brown's role in the G20 resulted in him being feted as the 2009 International Statesman by other world leaders, while Nobel prize-winning economist Paul Krugman described him as 'the saviour of the world economy', a tribute to Gordon Brown's success in leading the world out of the financial crisis.

A modern European response

It has become increasingly clear that the two most important countries in the next decade will be the US and China. But the European Union is the world's largest single market and the largest donor of international aid, operates the largest emissions trading scheme, and collectively spends more on defence than Russia or China – second only to the US. Europe will play a key role in responding to the shared challenges of the twenty-first century. A strong Britain in a strong Europe is the best way to preserve and advance our values and interests in the modern world.

The Labour government has put Britain at the heart of the European Union. As Foreign Secretary David Miliband argued recently, 'in everything from trade negotiations to the training of the Afghan police to sanctions on Iran or the greening of our economies, the European Union helps us achieve our foreign policy ambitions'. The EU is not a constraint if you have a government which knows how to wield influence.

A strong Europe is not an alternative to a strong British foreign policy, or to our special relationship with the United States, but it does mean recognising the critical role the EU can and must play in helping us meet our global challenges. Unless we pursue active engagement we cannot expect Europe to prioritise the things that matter most to us. So, from a practical and positive perspective the Labour government has chosen to play an active role in Europe and for the past thirteen years has helped shape the debate, benefiting from co-operation in areas including energy, climate change, enlargement, the economy and workers' and consumer rights.

This was particularly evident when Russia decided to turn off the gas supply in its dispute with Ukraine, affecting the supply of gas to the rest of Europe. Acting collectively, the EU ensured Russia resumed gas supplies promptly and reminded Russia of the importance of the European market. Acting alone, Britain would not have had that leverage.

The Labour government has also been at the forefront of pushing forward EU enlargement. Last year's twentieth anniversary of the fall of the Berlin Wall serves as a reminder of the incredible progress which has taken place in the last twenty years. The accession of countries such as Poland shows how far Europe has come by working together.

Being at the heart of Europe is demonstrably good for British business and the economy. The EU's internal market of nearly 500 million people, by far the largest in the world, creates huge opportunities for British businesses and consumers. This is crucially important for a trading nation like Britain, now the second biggest recipient of foreign direct investment in the world, with our exports worth well over £400 billion a year, 29 per cent of GDP.

Despite the benefits of being at the heart of Europe, David Cameron would marginalise Britain, leaving a question mark over his leadership capabilities and judgement. One of Cameron's first decisions as Conservative leader was to withdraw his party from the mainstream European People's Party, which includes Nicolas Sarkozy's Union for a Popular Movement and Angela Merkel's Christian Democratic Party. Instead he formed the new European Conservatives and Reformists Party with right-wing (and some far-right) parties in Poland, the Czech Republic and Latvia.

In forming this new group the Conservative Party has some extremely controversial allies. Polish MEP and member of the Conservatives' new grouping Urszula Kruper believes that the 'entire system for the reduction of carbon dioxide emissions is based on unproven hypotheses', while the leader of the Czech Republic's Civic Democrats has described climate change as a 'global myth'. The Conservative Party's Latvian partners took part in a march commemorating the Latvian SS. Their Polish partners, the Law and Justice Party, have members whose views on ethnic minorities and women would not be tolerated in mainstream political parties in the UK. David Cameron's Conservative Party wanted anti-European partners more than they wanted partners who held measured and progressive views on climate change and civil liberties.

Diplomacy requires being at the table and contributing to the debate. Europe is crucial for Britain's global influence. To bring China and the US to a deal on climate change in 2010 requires robust European leadership and commitment; while re-structuring the global economy requires European and internationally co-ordinated action. Failure to engage in Europe would leave us weaker and without a voice in areas critical to our future. Britain is better under a Labour government – taking seriously our international responsibilities and opportunities because it is in the British interest to do so.

Achieving more together than we can alone

On the back of the Labour Party membership card it says that 'we can achieve more together than we can alone'. This is true internationally as well as at home.

The world as we find it today, in which our interdependence is accelerating, speaks to the heart of Labour's modern internationalism: a foreign policy that favours engagement over isolation and with a role for Britain in shaping the world around us.

Whether it be fighting terrorism and nuclear proliferation, supporting economic development, alleviating poverty or tackling climate change our interests as a global community are bound up together. To build a more secure, stable, prosperous and fair world we need to win allies for our vision. To succeed requires leadership capable of fostering partnership and greater practical co-operation between nations. A Labour government will keep Britain at the heart of Europe and at the centre of international negotiations and decision-making. Labour is clear about Britains' identity, visions and values and positive about working with partners to achieve them.

Education sets us free

I joined the Labour Party because they are the political party that really cares about public services and society as a whole. I believe in an egalitarian society and the Labour Party reflects this view in its policies and actions. I am a proud supporter!

ALICE, CRYMYCH

Why education is so important for Labour

Since 1997 Labour's focus on education and in particular on schools sums up what the Labour Party stands for – giving everyone a fair chance in life. I believe that this government's greatest achievement is how the education of our young people has been transformed.

The importance of education to the Labour Party is summed up in this quote by Greek philosopher Epictetus, who claimed: 'Only the educated are free.' We have a moral responsibility to ensure that each person's talents are not wasted and to ensure that no barrier is allowed to hold people back – whether that is where they live, their parents' income and backgrounds or a special educational need or disability. A good education, more than anything else, can help people get on in life.

Education can also ensure that as a country we can compete in the global economy and attract jobs and investment to the UK. We can only do that if everyone has the skills and qualifications to make the most of their talents.

Markets alone will not achieve the education for all that is morally right and economically imperative. Labour wants to extend to all on middle and modest incomes the opportunity of the very best education, to create a fairer society. Creating a world class education system where every child goes to a good school, is taught well, achieves good qualifications and has the chance to fulfil their ambitions is no small goal but the Labour Party makes no apology for this bold vision.

The challenges Labour inherited

When Labour came to power in 1997 the British education system had suffered from decades of under-investment. We should not forget those leaking roofs, growing class sizes, and underpaid, unhappy teachers. Under the Conservatives, it seemed to be accepted that at the end of ten years of education two thirds of young people would leave school without five good GCSEs, with too many leaving with no qualifications at all. After leaving school, many young people would join Youth Training Schemes that provided limited opportunities but did take them off the youth unemployment statistics.

Reversing the damage done by eighteen years of Conservative government was always going to take time. Tony Blair's mantra of 'education, education, education' promised to make education the number one, two and three priorities. Labour made promises to parents and young people, and delivered on them:

- Labour said class sizes would be cut to thirty or under for five-, six- and seven-year-olds. In 1997 one third of 5–7-year-old children were taught in classes of more than thirty – now, only 2 per cent are.
- Labour promised free nursery places for all three- and four-year-olds. They have been delivered – and Labour is now increasing the entitlement and rolling out free nursery places to two-year-olds from poorer families.
- Labour committed to computer technology in the classroom. Computers are now integral to children's learning while teachers can expect to have an interactive whiteboard to aid their delivery.

- Labour was determined to modernise the comprehensive. The academies programme has certainly done this with over 200 new academies now open, often replacing under-performing schools.
- Labour promised to spend a higher proportion of the national income on education. That has been done too.

There have been fundamental improvements since 1997. Labour has put focus on the early years in a child's life, invested in teachers and teaching assistants, built new school buildings, and pursued this with a relentless focus on standards and results.

Early years education

If we are truly going to ensure that all young people have the chance to achieve their potential, we must ensure that from an early age, parents can access the support they need.

That is why Labour has put so much focus on Sure Start Children's Centres. Some 3,381 have opened since 1997 and anyone who has visited one knows what a difference they are making to children and their parents – as the story below from Louise makes clear. There will soon be more than 3,500 centres, one for every community. The Conservatives have said they want to change Sure Start from being a universal service for all families to one which only focuses on the poorest. While Labour has protected funding for Sure Start, the Conservatives have said they would cut funding by £200 million per year.

Louise, South London

My husband and I had recently moved into a new area, when I became pregnant with our first child. I did not know many people in the area, but knew that it would be really important for me to find local friends with young children. I attended ante-natal classes run by a team of midwives, and they told me about a new children's centre at my local school. After the arrival of our baby I went along, often calling in several times a week. I discovered a full range of activities that supported me and my baby – from support with breastfeeding, a midwife, rhyme time, stay and play sessions as well as a toy library full of fantastic learning toys to loan. The children's centre quickly became a focus in my life. It was invaluable as I made the transition into first-time motherhood.

Professionalising teaching

There are many more teachers and teaching assistants than there were in 1997. But just as importantly, Labour is investing in the skills and training of everyone who works with children. Investment and reform go in tandem, and together have transformed the teaching profession and the status of teaching. This story can be told by teachers much better than politicians. Mari Williams, an assistant principal at an academy in London, knows how far schools and teachers have travelled in the last decade.

Mari, London

They say that teachers are Wales's second greatest export – after water. Certainly there are a lot of teachers in my family including my grandmother and my mum, who was an infants' school head teacher. Despite the family tradition, I was certain of one thing when I was growing up – I was never going to become a teacher. It looked like a lot of hard work and stress, and teachers were not paid well and always being criticised.

I changed my mind because when Labour came to power in 1997 I began to have confidence that things were going to change. I wanted to do a job that made a difference. I was also sure that the Labour government was now going to help improve the status of the profession.

When I first started teaching, it was clear that schools had suffered from decades of under-investment. You bought your own coloured pencils for children and looked out for bargains at Woolworths. There was limited funding for trips or visits for students. This has changed dramatically in the last ten years. There is much less chance of leaking roofs and more chance that learning will be supported by state of the art computers, sports and arts facilities.

The government also introduced new pay thresholds to encourage teachers to stay in the classroom as well as the Advanced Skills Teacher programme, which pays excellent teachers to share their skills with others and remain at the chalkface. I really think that the status and standing of the profession has changed.

I am now fortunate enough to be part of the leadership team starting a new academy specialising in business and finance. We are in a fantastic state of the art building in inner city London. The new building sends a clear message to children that they matter and that their education is important. The school stands in place of another that was closed because only one in four pupils were leaving with good qualifications. Although we opened our doors just a few months ago I am confident about the future. In part that's because I have seen what this investment and focus has done at other schools: in August 2009 Mossbourne in Hackney announced that an incredible 84 per cent of students had achieved five good GCSE grades. This was possible because of a tireless focus on standards, high expectations of progress and excellent staff. It can be done.

Investment and buildings

Recruiting, training and retaining an excellent workforce is not without cost. In 1997 the government spent on average £3,030 for every pupil in England, compared with £6,350 this year. The proportion of national income spent on education has increased to 6.1 per cent, putting us joint first in Europe. But what does this mean in reality? This money has built, re-built or refurbished 4,000 schools, allowed us to employ 42,400 more teachers and increased the number of support staff by 212,000. Statistics tell a strong story but there is a lot more to how our schools have been improved. Ben is just one young man who remembers being taught in a crowded classroom in a school badly in need of investment and could not believe the change when he went in to collect his brother from school ten years later.

Ben, Ellesmere Port, Cheshire

I remember being a Year 4 pupil at primary school during the dying years of John Major's premiership. My class of over thirty children were taught in the 'mobile classroom', which was basically a large static caravan. This 'mobile classroom' was well designed for temporary use, but with a lack of funding to extend the school and rising numbers of pupils, it ended up being used for several years. It got hot in the summer and cold in the winter and it was always overcrowded. A teacher less talented than ours would never have coped with these conditions and our education and welfare could easily have suffered as a result.

Around ten years later, my little brother was a Year 4 pupil in the same school. When picking him up one day, I went into the classroom to have a look around. I was amazed – there were computers, a teaching assistant, all in a brand new, warm classroom given to a class of around twenty-four. Seeing my

brother in that environment really brought home to me what
politics is about – the new classroom, the teaching assistant
and the smaller class didn't just happen, they didn't just drop
out of the sky. When I think about what the difference between
Labour and the Tories really is, this is what I think about.

Standards

Labour has placed a relentless emphasis on standards and results,
because when you leave school it is your qualifications that take
you to the next step. Today, 80 per cent of eleven-year-olds reach
the expected level in English and 79 per cent in maths, compared
with 63 per cent for English and 62 per cent in maths in 1997. The
number of young people gaining five or more good GCSEs is up by
nearly 24 percentage points since 1997.

Sam became a school governor at a primary school four years
ago and is now chair. Sam, like many parents who are getting more
involved in their children's education, was impressed with what she
saw.

Sam, Leeds

I became a school governor four years ago, as I was keen to
be involved in making decisions that would help to shape the
future for my two daughters. At first I was apprehensive, unsure
of what bureaucracy and disillusionment I might find behind
the staffroom door. But it has been quite the opposite, my
school is full of dedicated, hard-working teachers. The changes
that I have seen support fantastic teaching with, whatever the
newspapers claim, minimal red tape. The best things for me are:
• One-to-one tuition guaranteeing additional support where
  needed in English and maths. This scheme was piloted
  initially and showed evidence of children making remarkable

progress. We have a number of booster classes at our school to make sure every child gets the support they need.

- The Stephen Lawrence Award has focused schools on equality and diversity – I feel particularly proud of my school's Level 2 achievement and I know the children get a huge amount from being involved.

- Vital improvements in safeguarding and child protection with inclusion high on the agenda, with greater emphasis on the role of our special educational needs co-ordinator.

- Healthy schools initiatives with a focus on healthy school meals and two hours of PE each week. Our school starts each day with Wake Up Shake Up, where the children and staff perform a dance routine which prepares them for a day of learning and is lots of fun too!

Everything that I have seen is an improvement for our children and I feel privileged to work in a robust and exciting education system.

The government is also supporting students as they move to their next steps. The educational maintenance allowance is something that I don't think many people know about – an unsung success story of the Labour government. It means that students who stay on at school or college after sixteen get a weekly payment for attendance. It has the effect of ensuring young people turn up every day and is targeted at those from lower-income backgrounds who need a bit of extra help paying for books, trips and the other costs of staying on at school or college.

What are the challenges now?

As competition in the economy intensifies it is even more important that all young people leave school ready for the world of work and with a love of learning.

The number of secondary schools below the minimum standards has gone from over half of schools in 1997 to just one in thirteen today. We are on track to ensure that every school is above the National Challenge benchmark of at least 30 per cent of students achieving five good GCSE grades, including in the vital subjects of English and maths, by 2011.

This is particularly important because a good education is the best route out of poverty and is the best way to unleash the talents of everyone in Britain. While the gap between the poorest pupils and the rest has narrowed under Labour, and while schools in the poorest areas have seen the fastest rises in results, the historic link between poverty and educational attainment remains. Of those children entitled to free school meals, only half achieve five or more good GCSEs, compared with just under three quarters of students who are not. University taster courses and summer schools targeting youngsters with little experience of higher education are also beginning to open up new opportunities to young people because until now only one in six students at top universities have come from lower socio-economic backgrounds. Breaking this historic link between social background and educational attainment remains the greatest challenge for Labour – as it has the potential to truly transform people's lives and is good for our economic success too.

We know that children do best when every school is an excellent place to learn with good discipline, a zero-bullying culture, high expectations and good results. While we know that the vast majority of young people want to do well, and the vast majority of parents provide the support that their children need, we must ensure that discipline is enforced for the sake of all students. That is why Labour has given teachers and head teachers extra powers to tackle bad behaviour and why it's legislating for tough Home School Agreements to enforce good discipline – so all pupils and parents take their responsibilities seriously. Labour is also working with alternative education providers, so that if a young person cannot participate in mainstream education – because of their behaviour, for example – they get the support they need so they do not drift into a life of anti-social behaviour and worklessness – better for the individual and the community.

Labour wants every young person to have the chance to get good qualifications, whether their strengths are practical, academic or both. That is why Labour has more than tripled apprenticeships and will provide education or training up to age eighteen for all children starting secondary school this year.

The new 14–19 years curriculum reflects a new diversity in education – with an increasing focus on tailoring education to the needs and aspirations of the individual student. At the heart of this are Labour's diplomas, combining theoretical and applied learning, which are our chance to break the historic divide between 'excellent' academic qualifications and vocational qualifications, which are seen as 'second class'.

Today's schools do not just have classrooms with rows of desks – increasingly schools have building workshops, engineering labs and design studios too. And young people are not only being taught in schools – there are many more partnerships with colleges and local businesses – so that education is geared around the needs of the student. And, because not everyone succeeds in education first time round and deserves a second chance to get the skills and qualifications they need to get on, Labour has supported learning in the workplace and for people who are out of work.

What will Labour do next?

Excellent head teachers supported by high-performing governing bodies, delivering a clear vision with a relentless focus on standards providing an education in state of the art schools with the latest technologies, can transform schools – and Labour's reforms are doing just that. A commitment to increasing the number of academies, protecting frontline schools spending and the focus on standards will continue to transform the education of more young people under Labour.

But, with budget constraints across government, investment over the next term has to be targeted where it is needed most.

Fiona Millar
Education campaigner, parent and governor

Many voters are either too young to remember what state schools were like thirteen years ago, or too old to know what they are really like now. The £37 billion (a 74 per cent increase in real terms) that Labour has poured into schools since 1997 has not been wasted, as the Tories like to argue. It has given us more children leaving primary school literate and numerate, more children with good GCSEs, better buildings, fewer failing schools and an increase in the number of children from the poorest homes going to university.

The gaps in attainment between the richest and poorest children are starting to narrow and we have yet to see the full benefit of so many Labour initiatives – no child over eleven has yet benefited from Sure Start, the universal entitlement to a free nursery place or the Child Trust Fund, for example.

Voters have a choice: to stick with a party that has shown a political and financial commitment to tackling the enormous challenge of educating all children, rich or poor, to a high standard, or to elect a party with a poor record on education in government and policies in the future that will undoubtedly undermine the good work of the past thirteen years.

Labour has a clear set of priorities. Every young person up to the age of eighteen will be guaranteed an apprenticeship or training – with a broader curriculum to meet the individual needs of young people. In secondary schools, Labour will provide a guarantee of one-to-one or small group tuition in English and maths for children who are falling behind. I know from when I was at school, some parents have long been able to support their children by providing private tuition and extra-curricular activities like music, drama and sport. Labour wants this privilege to be available to children whose families have modest and middle incomes too.

The Conservative approach

The Conservatives refuse to match Labour's pledge to protect school funding. They want immediate cuts to school funding because they have prioritised other things instead like their commitment to an inheritance tax cut which would give £200,000 to the 3,000 richest estates. And the Conservative Party have refused to match Labour's school leavers guarantee, which ensures that every young person who wants to stay in education or training at sixteen has a guaranteed and paid-for place in learning. The Conservatives' education policies would do nothing for children from families who are on modest or middle incomes – who want good local schools and support to get the qualifications and skills they need to fulfil their aspirations.

What the Conservatives do propose is that, regardless of local need and available places, parents with time on their hands should be given taxpayers' money to set up and run a new school for their children. But what about the vast majority of working parents who want a good local school for their children but do not have the time, energy or knowhow to set up their own school? In the Conservative 'age of austerity', this hugely expensive experiment can only be paid for by cuts to the budgets of every state school – indeed the Conservatives themselves say that they will scale back the Building

Schools for the Future programme, which is seeing thousands of schools re-built or refurbished, to pay for this expensive free-market experiment.

Labour does not believe in creating chances for a few lucky children, but believes in driving up standards for all children. If we are going to close the achievement gap between rich and poor, and make the most of everyone's skills and potential in what must be the opportunity economy of the future, then we must prioritise education for everyone and ensure that every child gets the qualifications they need to succeed.

Unlocking talents

Education, education, education – as true now as it was in 1997. Labour has proven that it is our top priority by investing in schools and teachers and by insisting on high standards. Education is the key to unlocking the talents of every young person, and to transforming our economy for the twenty-first century. Education can provide the opportunities which set each of us free. If you care about your child's education, your local school, and our future society, Labour is the party to make that difference.

A transformed National Health Service

I joined the Labour Party because I saw first hand the effects of a Tory government. My mum has worked in the NHS for over twenty-five years and I saw the damage the under-investment of Tory years did and the huge difference a Labour government made after 1997. The real differences that the Labour government made to ordinary people's lives in the NHS but also in education inspired me to join the party.

STEPHANIE, WEST MIDLANDS

A symbol of what Labour stands for

The NHS symbolises Labour's commitment to fairness, decency and equality. It is why Labour created the NHS in 1948 and why today it is working to make it more accessible and responsive to the needs of every patient. New hospitals, walk-in centres, better facilities and more choice have transformed the NHS since 1997.

Most recently, Labour has introduced new guarantees for patients – including the guarantee that you must wait no more than two weeks to see a specialist if you are suspected of having cancer. Survival rates from cancer have improved by over 18 per cent and the NHS now saves nearly 33,000 more lives from heart disease each year than it did before Labour came to power.

But reform must not stop. Under Labour, personalisation will be taken further so that the NHS meets our individual needs, prevention will move to the top of the agenda and new support and services for an ageing population will be the focus of Labour's reforms in this new decade. To back this up, Labour has committed that front-line NHS services will be protected from budget cuts.

The Conservatives failed to invest when they had the chance, and even now, when they claim to be the party of the NHS, there is clear antagonism among many in their party to the very concept of the NHS. Labour will never allow a return to an NHS where access to the best quality care was rationed and provided in outdated buildings, forcing many to use their savings to go private for life-saving treatment. Whether the Conservative Party now truly believes in the NHS is yet to be tested. It is a risk that we cannot afford to take.

Three stages of reform: investment

In 1997 the NHS was in decline. Patients waited eighteen months for operations or died waiting, and the sick were left unattended on hospital trolleys with too few doctors and nurses to care for them. Many asked whether the NHS was an anachronism.

Against this inheritance, Labour started a journey that would see investment in the NHS rise from £35 billion per year in 1997 to over £100 billion. The result: nearly 90,000 more nurses, 40,000 more doctors, over 100 new hospitals, around 100 walk-in centres, and over 650 one-stop primary care centres, providing excellent treatment and advice in all of our communities. One of the Conservatives' favourite soundbites is that Labour did not fix the roof while the sun was shining. In fact, Labour investment has built a new and much better roof over our hospitals and our schools.

We now have the shortest waiting times since records began. What was an average eighteen-month wait for hospital treatment is now a maximum of eighteen weeks from referral to treatment, with average waits even shorter. Death rates from cardiovascular disease for people under seventy-five are down by 44 per cent.

One man recently told me about how impressed he was after receiving a letter inviting him to hospital for routine surgery, just four days after his GP appointment. 'What a difference', he told me, 'compared to when I last needed to go in to hospital in 1995 – it took months to get an appointment and despite the best will of the doctors and nurses it was obvious that the place was falling apart.'

These achievements did not come without a fight. The Conservatives voted against Labour's investment, including opposing the one penny increase in National Insurance to get health spending up to the European average.

Kate, Michael and Eva, St Albans

Throughout my pregnancy, my husband and I were impressed with the standard of our local health services. We regularly saw one of two midwives located at our GP surgery, who were helpful, pleasant and extremely experienced. This was our first baby and so we had plenty of questions and worries. Davina and Margo were able to provide further information and quickly put us at ease.

I was lucky to have a healthy pregnancy and because we were given choices about what was right for us, we decided to opt for a home birth. During the birth we had fantastic support from the team of local midwives. There is no fooling anyone that childbirth is relaxing, but being in our own home, we were in a familiar and comfortable environment, in the knowledge that we had experienced and trusted help at hand.

We were supported by two midwives for the birth, and Margo, who we had seen throughout the pregnancy, looked after us for a few hours afterwards.

Eva is ten months now. She has certainly changed our lives. She is a happy and healthy and keeps us on our toes.

While increased investment was crucial, especially after years of neglect, Labour knows that investment without reform would not deliver the improvement in care that we needed. That is why Labour is changing the way the NHS works, giving patients more choice, involvement and power to personalise their treatment, and getting the best value for taxpayers.

Jo Brand, comedian

I want to talk about the NHS, which might be a bit odd because I haven't worked in it for twenty years. But when I did I witnessed the changes that came about via that champion of the poor, dispossessed and women, Margaret Thatcher. I worked in a 24-hour psychiatric emergency clinic in South London, which was all you might imagine it was. Through those years we saw auxiliary services farmed out to the lowest bidder, witnessed a shift in attitude which nominated our patients 'customers', and saw a creeping bureaucracy which favoured businessmen over experienced nurses to preside over the day-to-day workings of hospitals. I don't think the Tories are safe with hospitals and although there is much work to be done, I am still convinced that the NHS is only safe in the hands of a Labour government despite David Cameron's protestations on the glamorous posters I see all around me. I remember the *Hello Boys* posters for bras that legendarily made several male drivers crash. Well, if anything is going to make me drive into a tree, it's those Cameron billboards.

Three stages of reform: choice and personalisation

Labour is building a better NHS that offers personalised care, particularly for those with long-term conditions. Patient choice over treatment; individual control over services through personal budgets; and improved access through flexible evening and weekend opening times, walk-in centres and NHS Direct are all making a difference.

Lord Darzi's 2008 review of the NHS focussed on improving services so they are more responsive to our needs – this is now being driven forward locally with payment for quality and greater freedom for front line staff. 'Choose and Book' is also increasing choice and driving up standards, allowing us a choice of at least four hospitals and clinics for treatment – with information on how successful those hospitals are, as well as choice over the time and date of appointment, enabling people to fit in their health needs with work and family commitments much more easily. The NHS is increasingly meeting the individual needs of us all.

Personalised budgets for people with long-term conditions are also empowering people. I recently met a group of people with disabilities and their carers. Over coffee everyone was comparing personal health budgets and how they were using them to support their own needs. Two people with the same condition may have different needs and preferences on the way they are treated and supported. Labour is supporting people to live independent and individual lives – making the right choices, with the right information, for them and their families.

Dan, West London

I was born with cerebral palsy. I was three months premature and my parents spent weeks agonising over whether I'd make it. I survived thanks to the dedicated care of the team at Wolverhampton General Hospital, but the next few years were full of battles over therapy and schooling. The local health service, typical of the Tories at the time, wanted to stop my weekly physiotherapy sessions at the age of four. My family were outraged and we appealed the decision, and I told the appeal how important my therapy was. We won – and I kept receiving regular physiotherapy until I was sixteen. Fortunately, Labour ensures that people with disabilities don't have to fight for the services they deserve.

The local council (then Tory controlled) wanted to send me to a special school as that's where disabled kids went. My mum thought I was bright and fought for me to go to the local school. It was another battle, but I was the first disabled child to go there. A couple of years later, a girl with cerebral palsy followed and now nobody questions that disabled kids should go to the best local schools. Somebody called me a pioneer; I just thought it was common sense.

The extension of grants for students with disabilities helped me go to Exeter University. I got a 2:1 before studying for a Master's in History as well.

The change at our GP surgeries has also been radical, as Nicola's story tells us.

Nicola, London

We have a really lovely GP surgery, where the doctors have treated us since we moved here when I was pregnant with my six-year-old. They know us well now! They are open practically all day during the week, but not at weekends. Labour has opened up a polyclinic a couple of miles from us which is open seven days a week, 8 a.m. to 8 p.m. The Tories put out a load of ridiculous propaganda about these but I can't see how they can be anything other than brilliant for families like ours. Our own doctors' surgery is always really manic on a Monday after the weekend, and it can be hard to get appointments that fit around our work commitments and school hours, but this new clinic means we can go there any time we like and see a doctor, but still stay on our family doctor's books. The NHS is absolutely fantastic

> now – I remember so well how horrendous the NHS was under the Tories, with people waiting years for crucial operations.

Over three quarters of all GP practices now offer extended opening hours, allowing patients to access care when it's convenient for them. But increasingly, you do not have to go to the doctors to get expert advice. One of the most exciting innovations in the last decade has been NHS Direct – providing support for patients via the internet or telephone, twenty-four hours a day, seven days a week, across the country, answering about five million calls a year. But despite the difference it has made, NHS Direct is one of the services that will feel the cold hand of the Conservatives' age of austerity – it is set to be cut if they win the election.

Dr Neil Goulbourne, Coventry

As with so much Tory policy, Cameron's plans for the NHS amount to a combination of insignificant meddling and unachievable soundbites. To the eyes of a GP like me, the most ill-considered proposal is to force family doctors to manage the entirety of their patients' budgets, which would entail commissioning their hospital care. Not only has this been heavily criticised by the British Medical Association as unworkable, it's a policy that can hardly be described as change for a Conservative Party that introduced something similar [GP fund holding] when it was last in government. The Tories' draft health manifesto provides ample evidence of the brazen shallowness of Cameron's offer to voters.

Three stages of reform: guarantees

Because of Labour's investment and the increase in standards, it is now possible to move beyond the centralised target framework that was necessary to ensure an improvement in performance post-1997, to an era where patients have new guarantees.

The NHS Constitution, introduced by Labour, has already enshrined the principle of access to health services based on need, not ability to pay. It has turned access to all approved health treatments into a right, and has begun to set out what patients should expect if quality is not met.

These new guarantees include patients suspected of having cancer being seen by a specialist within two weeks, or their doctor having to secure them an immediate appointment at another hospital. It also includes patients being treated at hospital within eighteen weeks after first seeing their GP, and fast-tracked if they have a serious condition. And everyone aged 40–74 will have the right to free health checks, as the NHS moves to a new prevention-led era. These guarantees give people the peace of mind that if they or their family get ill, they will be treated quickly, effectively – and for free. The Conservatives will not commit to any of these guarantees – not even the one for cancer.

Tracey, Barnsley

In 2007, aged thirty-five and with three young children, I was diagnosed with breast cancer.

I saw my GP on Monday and as there was definitely something there, he referred me for further investigation, as an urgent case. That same day, I had a mammogram, an ultrasound examination and five core biopsies. There were no delays, just staff who regularly came to check if there was anything I needed. Just a week later, my results were ready. I had cancer.

I immediately saw a specialist breast-care nurse and the surgeon who would be doing the operation that I needed – a radical mastectomy. I was put under no pressure but asked for it to be done as soon as possible, so less than a week later I was admitted to hospital for surgery. Just three weeks and five days after finding it, my cancer was removed.

My stay in hospital following surgery was comfortable and my care was thorough. My husband was also able to stay with me as late as he wanted to – I was grateful for that as it was a very traumatic time and I really needed him to be around.

It was exactly the same with my after-care: thorough attention, absolute dignity and respect from start to finish.

I was treated in Barnsley Hospital NHS Trust. The NHS is Labour's greatest achievement. It saved my life, and the government's two-week cancer care guarantee is vital. The NHS staff made the experience easier to bear. They are heroes and I thank them every single day, when I look at my children and appreciate being alive.

New challenges

Labour investment, choice, personalisation and guarantees have transformed the treatment our families receive. But the NHS must also meet new challenges. The battle at the election is not just to preserve the reforms that Labour has made and the guarantees that have been introduced. The battle is to ensure that the NHS adapts to meet the new needs of an ageing society, supports us to live healthier lives, and provides us with the help we need to manage long-term conditions – particularly those most affected by poor health.

Luke, Hackney

Last year I went from being a healthy 36-year-old to being suddenly seriously ill and in a wheelchair. I developed a very rare illness – a bone marrow tumour put antibodies into

my blood which attacked my nervous system, leaving me
unable to walk and with very weak hands and arms. The
NHS was fantastic. From the moment I arrived in A&E at
my local hospital, Homerton University Hospital, I got first-
class treatment and care. I spent five months, including two
months of intensive rehabilitation, at the National Hospital for
Neurology and also had radiotherapy at University College
Hospital. I can't thank the doctors and nurses, physios
and occupational therapists, but also cleaners, drivers and
porters, enough. They always treated me with respect,
compassion and friendship.

The personal care I got made life bearable even when I was
very weak and in a terrifying situation. Since I left hospital the
care I've received hasn't stopped: I've had two physiotherapy
sessions every week, helping to get me walking again, I have
also been provided with all the kit and adaptations I needed to
live life normally, even getting help paying for transport to work.
As a patient I have experienced a system that we should all be
very proud of. The NHS was created by Labour and opposed
by the Tories. Tory MEP Daniel Hannan is still attacking it. I
think it embodies Labour values of solidarity and community.

Long term care for the elderly

The fastest growing challenge in the health service is how we care for
our older people in ways that preserve their dignity and independence.
I have seen the challenges first hand with my grandparents, who have
Alzheimer's. The decisions that families have to make for elderly
relatives are so difficult, and often heart-breaking. My grandparents,
married for over fifty years, now live apart because their needs are so
acute, but different, that they have to be in separate care homes. The
toll it takes on those nearest to them is also high. My mum retired as a
head teacher because the challenges of her job could not be combined

with visiting both her parents in different homes in different London suburbs – or with the stress and sadness of it all.

It is clear that the care system needs reforming. That is why Labour has proposed the National Care Service to provide more and better care for people in their own homes – making services available not just to those who can afford them, but to the hard-working majority too. The recent Personal Care at Home Bill is the first step in setting up the National Care Service, and will guarantee free personal care at home to over a quarter of a million people with the most critical care needs, including the frail and elderly, and protect the savings of 166,000 people who currently get free care from future charges.

These changes will make a huge difference, to those who need more help as they get older and to the people who love them and care for them.

Prevention and health inequalities

Labour is also committed to the prevention and early detection of illness – because we will all have more fulfilling lives if we are healthy and well, and because it can reduce the pressure on frontline NHS services.

I am on the board of a Healthy Living Network in Leeds. The charity's aim is to improve the health of people in the most deprived communities. We have funding to run a fruit and vegetable stall in estates and community centres, a pub quiz and beer mats on men's health (amazingly popular and testament to the fact that not everyone wants to go to the doctors to get health advice), fitness classes for people recovering from strokes and other conditions, and much more. These are excellent examples of the voluntary sector and government working together in the local community. The focus will increasingly be on targeted, bespoke services like this in the years ahead.

Probably the biggest difference Labour has made to public health is to ban smoking in public places – saving hundreds of thousands of lives through fewer cases of cancer, heart disease and strokes. Combined with the ban on tobacco advertising and new NHS Stop Smoking services this has resulted in the proportion of adults smoking dropping from 28 per cent to 22 per cent since 1998.

I was speaking recently to a young woman who has been smoking since she was fourteen. She welcomed the smoking ban because it would be a good deterrent for her and would stop other young people from taking up the habit. She has just got her free NHS Stop Smoking pack and her new year's resolution is to be smoke free by the end of 2010 – saving £35 a week and possibly her life.

While the Conservatives speak about tackling health inequalities, their promises ring hollow. When Labour passed measures to remove cigarettes from counter displays and vending machines, to discourage young people from taking up smoking, the Conservatives voted against them – saying that government should not meddle. Labour has made tough decisions and taken on vested interests to improve the health and life chances of all, especially those from low income backgrounds, who are more likely to be smokers. Can the Conservatives really be serious about tackling health inequalities when they did not support even these straightforward measures to improve health outcomes?

Labour has improved the NHS for everyone, and this has particularly helped the least well off, who never had the choice to go private. Health inequalities – where you are more likely to die or be ill if you are poor – are the worst kind of injustice that Labour policies have worked hard to tackle, channelling resources and support to the areas with the worst health outcomes. The results are heart disease deaths down a third more in those areas than in the country as a whole, with smoking and teenage pregnancies down too.

While we should welcome the Conservatives' proclaimed conversion to tackling inequalities, in practice it is unclear how it fits with their plan to scrap the Department of Health and devolve decisions on spending. National strategies have made a huge difference in the last few years, especially in reducing cancer among groups most at risk, including among people on low incomes. Would the Conservatives maintain these strategies that have made such a difference? While the Conservatives have started to talk the talk on health, they do not have the policies, or the values, to protect and improve the NHS.

Safe in whose hands?

The NHS represents everything Labour stands for. Labour created the NHS and Labour rescued the NHS after two decades of chronic under-investment so that today it is the institution that the British people are most proud of. Now Labour has reformed the NHS to increase choice and personalisation and to get better value from the increased resources. But we must also judge a party on where it is going, and in health the challenge is clear – we must rise to the challenge of better long-term care for the elderly. Labour has set out its vision and if re-elected will build a National Care Service for the twenty-first century as Clement Attlee and Aneurin Bevan built the NHS in the aftermath of the Second World War. Labour is the only party of the NHS; it is only safe in Labour's hands.

Poverty is preventable

I joined the Labour Party because I was proud of what we have done since 1997: 500,000 children have been lifted out of poverty, a National Minimum Wage was introduced and we lead the global campaign to write off the debt for the world's poorest nations.

ALI, LONDON

Introduction

Despite the recession, Britain is undoubtedly a rich country. Compared with much of the world, standards of living and opportunity are high. But beneath the affluence poverty remains.

Poverty is a waste of human talent and it is a waste to society. It is also a question of fairness – it's not right that our life chances depend on our parents' wealth or income. Liberating talent, unlocking potential and tackling hardship will make for a better and fairer Britain. The purpose of the Labour Party is to bring the life chances of the most fortunate in our society within the grasp of everyone, pursuing a belief that a more equal society is better for us all. Opportunity and security should be extended, so everyone has the chance of a decent life.

The government defines poverty as a family living on less than 60 per cent of median earnings. What poverty means, for a child, is that they cannot have birthday parties or go on school trips. It may even mean they have to forgo a winter coat. It will also mean overcrowding at home, less space to do homework and to play. Growing up in poverty means poorer health, less chance of getting a well-paid job, more chance of being unemployed. It also often means the absence of things that make life enjoyable.

The passion at the heart of the Labour Party has always been to alleviate poverty and extend opportunities. Sidney and Beatrice Webb and the Fabians saw the slums of East London and wanted to do something about them, the trade unions campaigned for better protection for hard-working men and women, while Keir Hardie stood for Parliament to press for a minimum wage and full employment. In post-war reconstruction, the Labour Party set out its vision for a welfare state to eradicate Beveridge's five giants of disease, idleness, squalor, ignorance and want: sixty years on the NHS remains the vanguard of a state that respects and empowers all of its citizens. Extending opportunities and reducing poverty remain Labour's passion today.

What has been achieved?

In 1997, 2.9 million pensioners were living in poverty and 3.4 million children lived in poverty, a number which had doubled since 1979. Facing the stark inequalities inherited from previous Conservative governments, Labour has fought the differences in opportunities that start at the cradle and continue to the grave. Since Labour came to power, around 500,000 children and 900,000 pensioners have been lifted out of poverty and Labour has committed to abolish child poverty by 2020.

For people in work – and 57 per cent of working-age adults living in poverty are in households where at least one person is in work – the minimum wage has ensured a basic income matched with protection at work. Tax credits have also made a big difference in tackling in-work poverty. Available to 90 per cent of families with children and over one million people without, tax credits have come into their own during the recession, with 400,000 people who have seen a fall in their income getting extra support averaging £37 a week.

Kate Green, former chief executive of the Child Poverty Action Group

In 1999, when Tony Blair pledged that Labour would end child poverty in a generation, the UK had the highest rate of child poverty in the EU. Today 500,000 fewer children are in poverty, and Britain no longer languishes at the foot of the European league table.

Across the country, this is one of Labour's most valued achievements – not least because most families have benefited from policies such as tax credits and increases in child benefit. What's more, poverty is costly for all of us – children who grow up poor suffer poorer health, worse educational outcomes and a poorer-quality childhood. That is a waste of a child's future potential, expensive for our public services, and I am absolutely certain it isn't fair.

Despite progress over the past ten years, there's still a long way to go to reduce child poverty in this country to the levels of the best in Europe, let alone to eradicate child poverty by 2020 as pledged by Blair. The evidence is clear about what has worked: redistributive fiscal policy, decent jobs and investment in public services have underpinned our progress to date. Now, as the country emerges from recession, those are the policies we must accelerate. Ending child poverty requires that economic growth and reducing inequality go hand in hand.

Labour's policies have also supported pensioners. The poorest third of pensioner households are now on average £2,100 better off than they would have been without significant changes to tax credits. The introduction of the winter fuel allowance and the minimum income guarantee have all made a difference.

Eileen, Bromborough

I retired several years ago with a small works pension. My husband died in 1966 so I managed to work and bring my daughter up. But in retirement I was much worse off.

When pension credit was introduced it changed everything. Not just the extra bit of money but everything that went with it. In some ways the things that mean most to me are the most straightforward – a free TV licence and bus pass (and I use it a lot), and the winter fuel allowance. I worked hard all my life, and it's only the actions of the Labour government that have made sure I'm comfortable in retirement.

Tackling the causes of poverty

Tackling poverty means tackling its causes, not just its symptoms. Those causes are many and varied. Poor skills and qualifications, having a disability or a family member with a disability, living in an area with high levels of unemployment, a lack of affordable childcare, and struggling to bring up a family alone can all be part of the cause. The solutions are not straightforward and it takes time, and sustained commitment, to make a difference. It's not a case of telling people to pull up their socks, incentivising marriage, or decrying broken Britain. If it were, the battle to end poverty would have been won by now.

Recognising that the impact of poverty starts early in life, Labour introduced Sure Start centres and free nursery places to ensure that every child has the best start, offering a host of opportunities to young families from every walk of life. The early years when a child's development is so fundamental can make all the difference throughout a school career and beyond. In the Sure Start centres I have visited, mums are offered careers support, training, English and computer courses and much more. The centres have made a real difference across the country, transforming some communities where families had once been isolated.

Angela, Lancashire

At forty-six years old I wrote my first ever letter to a political party, to Labour, to thank them for all the help they have given my family. As a single mother I was struggling without any financial support from my ex-husband for years. However, with child benefit, tax credits, the CSA and housing benefit from Labour my family is much better off. With the extra money I can now afford for my children to attend a whole host of sporting and musical coaching sessions. They also attend lots of free out-of-school activities in my area such as football, singing, drama and exercise classes. My children aren't lazy or troublesome hoodies or out causing trouble, as I am able to provide them with lots of great activities and pastimes to keep them interested and active and it's all thanks to the Labour Party – they have made a real difference.

Beyond the early years, record investment in schools and increasingly demanding standards have driven up educational attainment, while the Educational Maintenance Allowance has opened up sixth forms to people who may not otherwise have been able to afford it.

Labour has also increased the number of university places and widened opportunities. The Aim Higher scheme, which encourages school pupils – especially those without a family history of higher education – to consider university, has opened up the prospect of university education to students who would otherwise have no idea about what further study might entail or offer. Recent measures will offer bursaries to 10,000 undergraduates taking internships, an important link to employment and especially valuable to those who do not have the connections to give them a helping hand into the right job.

Bryony, Leeds

When I started my A-levels in 2003, I was painfully aware of the extra financial burden this could place on my mum as well as how expensive it was simply to get to college, what with books, bus fares, pens, paper and a whole myriad of other costs. I suddenly found that I needed to spend money to be able to keep up with my classes properly. Fortunately, I qualified for £30 a week in Educational Maintenance Allowance. While for many people that might not seem like a lot, to me it made the world of difference. I would have had to work an extra 7½ hours every week at my part-time job to make that £30, which is a lot when you're sixteen and trying to study for A-levels. The EMA made life a lot easier, took away a great deal of worry and eased the financial burden at home. A lot of my friends also benefited from the scheme, without which many of us would not have survived two years at college and made it into university. It would have simply been too expensive.

We can see the difference that Sure Start and investment in schools has made, and the benefits will also be felt in the future: the first toddlers to benefit from Sure Start will be eighteen in 2017, while chances offered by record investment in schools will be reaped for years to come. The biggest achievement of the last thirteen years has been the proof that government can make a difference, education can be revolutionised and the welfare state improved to give everyone new opportunities to flourish. The Labour government is tackling poverty and the root causes of poverty, and will continue to do so.

Mark Law, CEO, Barca-Leeds

Working alongside some of the most vulnerable members of our community in the 1980s and 1990s, it was clear we needed a seismic shift in public policy if we were to have any chance of lifting people out of an overwhelming sense of hopelessness. Many of the families we were working with were experiencing multi-generational worklessness, and many were facing difficulties with mental health, addiction and poverty.

Labour's win in 1997 brought a new sense of optimism. Within a year we had begun to employ young people under the New Deal and were working on establishing Sure Start locally. We were responding to youth crime through the establishment of a Youth Inclusion Project; we established new organisations, including a Healthy Living Network; we began to develop targeted advice and guidance through Connexions; and we began to join things up, working with the whole family, supporting schools to think outside the box and working in partnership with all children's services.

Today we employ over a hundred staff who engage with over 2,000 people a week. Under Labour we have been able to have a more positive impact upon people's lives and have made a difference for the whole community.

We have come a long way, but with children and pensioners still living in poverty, there is clearly more to do. That is why Labour has introduced the Child Poverty Bill, enshrining the commitment to eradicate child poverty in law. This is the commitment of the Labour government – it is opposed by the Conservative Party.

Poverty and the financial crisis

In a recession, the poorest families suffer most. Those on low incomes often have low skills so getting a new job is not always easy and low income families have fewer savings on which to draw in harder times. Labour has taken direct action to limit the impact of the recession, protecting those least responsible for the crisis, helping families stay in their homes and people to stay in jobs. Child tax credit increases were also brought forward by a year, to benefit nearly four million families, and employers have been offered a £1,000 incentive to recruit people who are long-term unemployed. These measures are evidence of Labour's commitment to stop the recession from undermining progress towards the goal of ending poverty – and they must be sustained.

Andy Flannagan, singer-songwriter and director of the Christian Socialist Movement

I got into politics because I wanted to follow the biblical injunction to 'speak up for those who cannot speak for themselves'. Multinational companies and media moguls will always have multi-million pound budgets for their PR departments to make sure their side of the story is told. Labour can give a voice to those who are without that resource, yet equally deserving of representation. With a globalised financial market, this has never been more important, as recent events have made painfully clear. Only Labour has the understanding and gut instinct on policy to favour the people who most need support, getting beyond mere charity to justice.

Global events also affect poverty. As the cost of oil has risen, so too have fuel costs. Pensioners and low income families face a hard choice in the face of these rises, whether to spend the money that is needed to heat their homes or to buy other essentials. The winter fuel allowance, raised to as much as £400 for those over eighty years, makes sure that homes are heated to the extent needed, not the extent that can be afforded, while schemes to provide better insulation in social housing are ensuring that fuel bills are as low as possible. I spoke to one pensioner during the 'big freeze' in January, who had just received £100 in extra cold weather payments. She told me how fantastic it was that she could turn up the fire without worrying whether she could afford to. Before the allowance she had struggled to heat the house she had lived in for fifty years.

Poverty is persistent

It is hard to break cycles of worklessness and poor educational attainment in families and communities. Of course it is frustrating that despite progress, thirteen years into a Labour government poverty persists. It is hard to comprehend that some have so much while some have so little. But although I am adamant that poverty is preventable, I realise that there is no simple panacea – we must persist if we are to succeed.

The educational attainment of children from families who are unemployed is five times lower than families in work. The chances of the son or daughter in social class five reaching social class one are thirty-two times lower than the chances of the son or daughter of someone in social class one staying there. Entering into the 'professions' also depends largely on the sort of family you are born into. The typical journalist or accountant of the future will today be growing up in a family better off than three in four of all families in the UK.

Living in poverty also means extra costs for those who can least afford them – the poverty premium. Over the course of a year, a poor family can expect to pay up to £1,000 extra for goods, services and credit. A cooker purchased on store credit can cost double the price of one paid for up front. A gas bill paid on a pre-payment meter is approximately 10 per cent higher than one paid by direct debit.

These costs pile on top of higher insurance premiums, paying to cash cheques and get cash out, or simply to get the shopping home. Poverty often means little access to a bank account or bank loans, so the use of doorstep lenders and loan sharks is higher among the poor too. This poverty premium compounds the everyday difficulties of living on a low wage.

Labour will continue to champion the alleviation of poverty and should be judged against its achievements in doing so. As Harold Wilson said, Labour 'is a moral crusade or it is nothing'.

Benefits of a more equal society

Poverty has fallen sharply under Labour, but there is more to do to create a society where opportunities are more fairly distributed. Poverty is unfair and too great a degree of inequality can threaten social integration and breed division in our communities.

Society as a whole suffers from inequality, not just those who are poor. In a groundbreaking study published last year, Wilkinson and Pickett in *The Spirit Level* show that it is not just families who live in poverty that suffer when the rich and the poor live totally different lives. Testing the impact of inequality between and within countries, they found that more equal societies almost always do better.

A more equal society generates an atmosphere of trust and inclusion, of community cohesion. Inequalities emphasise the differences between people and isolate us from one another. A government that fights for greater equality fights for better health, lower crime and a stronger economy. The Labour government over the last thirteen years has fought for greater equality, demanding better standards in the workplace, minimum pay, more early years support, a fairer income in retirement, and better schools and hospitals. The change is being made, and the long-term benefits of the measures introduced will affect us all if they are sustained.

Supporting families on modest
and middle incomes

Families on modest and middle incomes have all been affected by
the recession. It is right that all families, not just the very poorest,
get the support they need to help them through difficult times. The
welfare state and public services are there, and must always be there,
for all of us when we need them most. At key moments, like having
children, falling ill, retiring, needing long-term care, or losing your
job, we all rely on the welfare state and public services.

A welfare state that supports us all also improves the standard
of public services for people who need them most. As Richard
Titmuss warned, 'services for the poor have always tended to be
poor services'. Universal public services build solidarity between
us – we all pay in and we can all draw on support when we need
it. Strong public services and mutual support are what helps make
Britain a strong and civilised society.

But while Labour believes that families on middle incomes
should get the support they need, not just to get by, but to get on,
the Conservative Party wants to leave them to go it alone. Under
a Conservative government, tax credits would be abolished for all
families earning more than £31,000. The Child Trust Fund would
not benefit your child unless you earned less than £16,000. And
Sure Start would not be for every family, in every community, but
would only be available for the very poorest.

The Conservatives, instead of targeting money at children, say
that the answer to poverty is to support marriage. While everyone
would prefer it if children were bought up by two loving parents,
that is not always the reality – for all sorts of reasons. Penalising
a mother or father if their husband or wife dies or leaves them
is hardly family friendly. Conservative policies would not benefit
the most vulnerable children, reduce poverty or give support to
those most in need of it. Instead of prioritising families on modest

and middle incomes, and tackling child and pensioner poverty, the Conservative Party are insistent on protecting the privileges of a minority – raising the inheritance tax threshold rather than channelling support to families.

Fairness at the core

While the Conservatives say poverty is the fault of 'broken Britain', Labour recognises its more nuanced causes. The recession has shown that markets don't have all the answers. But government, when motivated to act with and on behalf of the people, can support the young person at risk of being the next generation of long-term young unemployed, the mum who wants to work and support her family, and the pensioner who is worried about heating his home. Labour is on the side of people with modest and middle incomes – determined to eliminate the poverty that still scars too many families, pensioners and communities.

Fairness is at the heart of the measures Labour has taken since 1997, it has been at the heart of measures to combat the recession, and it will continue to be at the heart of policies that go beyond the downturn. Government can and should offer protection from the excesses of markets, supporting people when they need it most.

Strong and stable communities

I joined the Labour Party because it stands for everyone regardless of their financial assets, marital status, ethnic origins or religious beliefs. I think this is the fairest way to run a country and so I want to do my bit to ensure that a fair party which stands for everyone is voted in this year.

JOSH, COALVILLE

Building strong communities

Communities are the arena in which policies are played out, and strong social bonds are the platform on which we will build a stronger, fairer and more successful Britain. A strong economy goes hand in hand with a strong society, and communities are integral for the economic recovery too – building local strategies for regeneration and jobs.

The Labour vision is that wherever we live and whoever we are, we can access the things that make our lives fulfilling, including decent housing, a sense of belonging and community, arts, sport, open spaces and culture.

But building these communities is not a matter of chance or luck. If nobody provides and looks after our parks and green spaces, then you cannot hold the summer fayre; if nobody supports our community centres and sports grounds, then residents' meetings and football training cannot happen; and if nobody polices our area, then vandals are free to destroy our environment. These are things that the market cannot provide. But local communities, working with central and local government, can provide the shared facilities that make life more fulfilling.

David Cameron decries a 'broken Britain'. But while all

communities face challenges, his criticisms do not do justice to the energy, community spirit and sense of pride that exists in the vast majority of our neighbourhoods. And, while he insists on doing down Britain, he has no coherent view of how to 'fix' society. Instead, Cameron's hands-off approach would leave people on their own, accentuating the gaps between rich and poor, wasting potential. The results of the Conservatives' hands-off dogma were seen in the 1980s and are seen now in their policies and prescriptions for modern Britain.

Homes and families

Communities start with families. And the first need for our families is a home where we feel safe and secure. Labour has helped more families achieve the aspiration of home ownership. Through the recession the government has also helped more families stay in their homes – limiting the number of home repossessions that became synonymous with the recession of the early 1990s.

But for many people, owning their own home is out of reach, or is not possible straight away. Because of this, and because the quality and security of private rented accommodation is not always of a high standard, social housing is hugely important.

In 1997, the number of council houses had fallen from a peak of five million in 1976, to 3.4 million. With £19 billion worth of outstanding repairs on council housing, and huge backlogs, many families and pensioners were living in poor housing – with the impact that has on health and well-being. Clearing this backlog was a priority – getting more social homes up to the standard that most of us would take for granted. By this year, the government will have got 92 per cent of homes up the decency standard. I can see the difference in my area. New bathrooms, kitchens, windows and doors that keep out the cold. Not too much to ask, but a huge improvement for thousands of families and pensioners.

Since Gordon Brown became Prime Minister, the largest house building programme for over two decades, worth over £500 million, has started. Over 4,000 will be built in 2010, providing new, low carbon, family homes.

With innovative new policies, Labour has managed to bring home ownership within the reach of more families and young people. Shared ownership schemes have allowed people to part own and part rent their home, buying a bigger share over time when they can afford to. This flexibility can help reduce the divide between the 'haves' and 'have nots' in the housing market.

Gemma, Tower Hamlets

After university, I moved to a rented flat in London. I loved living in the city but the place was tiny. I lived in a couple of rented places with friends but last year I bought on a shared equity scheme. I have a mortgage on 30 per cent and the housing association owns the other 70 per cent – which I pay rent on. I've been able to decorate it as I want and I don't have to deal with agents or landlords.

The real benefit for me has been the security, knowing that this is my home and I can set down some roots in the local area, instead of looking for somewhere new each year.

I just couldn't have got a mortgage for 100 per cent of a place. The shared equity scheme has given me a chance to get on the ladder and get the benefits of home ownership.

The Conservatives have fought against Labour's home-building programmes, urging council leaders to block developments, pulling up the ladder that would enable first-time buyers to realise their dream of owning their own home. It's not just first-time buyers who the Conservatives are failing to support. In councils controlled by the Conservatives, including Hammersmith and Fulham, measures such as raising social rents to market levels and ending secure tenancies have been proposed, which would be most damaging to the oldest and most vulnerable in our society.

As new homes are built, Labour has been re-assessing how social housing is allocated, to ensure fairness for local people. If someone has lived in an area for their whole life, they should have a chance to live there when they start their own family – near to friends and family and with access to their local community networks. The Labour government has ensured that local authorities can now give priority to local people in the allocation of social housing. This is fair and it will support the mainstream majority – on modest and middle incomes – up and down the country.

It is also right that everyone who lives in a council house should work if they are able to. Community re-generation schemes, coupled with work by Jobcentre Plus, means that everyone should be offered support back to work and must work if they can – as set out in chapter three.

Cities transformed

As the Labour government builds the communities of the future, it is building on the success story of the regeneration of our cities. Cities, including many northern cities, which had been in long-term decline, have been re-energised from what they had become in the 1980s and early 1990s – providing jobs, cultural experiences and boosting the economy.

Tom Bloxham MBE, Chairman, Urban Splash

The last thirteen years have seen amazing changes in our cities; whether in Manchester, Newcastle, Birmingham or Bristol we've see the regeneration of our city centres.

> Urban decay and urban blight have been replaced by new and restored buildings. We've reversed the exodus from our cities and people and jobs have moved back into the centres; and galleries, concert halls, museums and restaurants have all opened.
>
> I've seen first hand the incredible role culture has played in revitalising city centres with the Manchester International Festival and Liverpool Capital of Culture.
>
> I'm incredibly proud of the changes we have seen and the amazing city centres we've helped create. All of this has been made possible by successful partnerships between government, local authorities and progressive private companies like Urban Splash. However, the job is not finished and there is still real deprivation around the edge of our cities. We all need to continue working together over the next years to finish the job we've started.

Safe and secure neighbourhoods

Strong communities depend on common values and fair rules. Hard-working families must know that tough action will be taken against those who break the rules and give nothing back. That is why Labour has taken tough and necessary measures to combat crime and anti-social behaviour.

From 1979 to 1997 crime doubled, while the number of convictions fell by a third. The chances of being a victim of violent crime increased by 61 per cent, and the chances of being a victim of burglary nearly trebled. Labour promised to be 'tough on crime, and tough on the causes of crime'.

Since 1997 crime has fallen by 36 per cent. More offenders are brought to justice each year, with dangerous criminals more likely to go to prison and stay there for longer. Spending on law and order is 40 per cent higher, helping pay for nearly 17,000 more police officers and 16,800 new community support officers compared to 1997.

Anti-social behaviour should not be tolerated – we all rightly expect to live in neighbourhoods free from the corrosive effects of intimidation and harassment. In the last thirteen years new tools and powers, including anti-social behaviour orders, dispersal orders and premises closure orders, have been made available to the police. While there is still a lot of work to do to tackle anti-social behaviour, a lot has been achieved. Labour will continue to provide the police with the powers they need to support our local communities.

Ruth, police community support officer, West Yorkshire

I've been a police community support officer for six years now, and for the last five years I've been in the Safer Neighbourhoods Team. During this time I've seen massive changes – but most importantly we've made huge in-roads in tackling anti-social behaviour. The government has given the police and PCSOs new powers – as well as the famous ASBOs, we've now got non-association and exclusion orders. These are really helpful when we've got gangs causing problems in a neighbourhood.

There have also been big improvements in witness protection – this has helped to build up the trust of local people, and also to catch and prosecute more criminals.

When I have a rare week off, I am always heartened when I return to the beat to know that I've been missed. I'm part of the local community and I love my job. There is always more to do, but we've now got the resources and the tools to tackle anti-social behaviour in our communities.

The introduction of neighbourhood policing teams, police

community support officers and community wardens has successfully transformed many of our communities, as Pat's story shows.

Pat, community warden, Leeds

In 2004 I became a community warden in an estate that one national newspaper described as the worst estate in Britain. But, although there were problems, there were also fantastic opportunities. With the support of our local councillors we got money to do up the community centre and make it the hub of the community. We now run keep-fit classes, jobcentre sessions, debt advice, community meetings, mums and tots groups and much, much more.

Every day I am out and about on the estate. I work with the local rugby club to provide after-school and holiday activities for the kids. I liaise with the police and community support officers to ensure that no one is the victim of bullying or anti-social behaviour. And I go and visit families who need a bit of extra help and pensioners living alone to make sure they are OK.

My job is enormously varied. I hope – and think – that I make a difference to the whole community. Things are definitely improving around here thanks to Labour's investment in our area and local people. Labour hasn't given up on communities like mine.

Despite the recession and pressures on budgets, Labour has ring-fenced spending on frontline police, and has committed to maintain neighbourhood policing. The Conservatives have not matched this promise. Instead, they want to cut back on CCTV cameras and opposed new powers for police to take DNA and fingerprint evidence – measures that have been hugely successful in catching and punishing criminals.

Secure borders

We all need to know that our country's borders are secure. No government has been completely successful in convincing the public that immigration is managed well. But I believe that Labour's tough and fair policies will produce the necessary balance of strengthening our borders while allowing access to people who will benefit our economy or who seek asylum.

The UK Borders Agency, introduced in 2008, combined with better enforcement of decisions made by the Home Office, means that more people are being sent home or are denied entry to the UK. New border controls have also been introduced that will count non-European migrants in and out of the country. These are the measures that the last Conservative government started to dismantle in 1994. Identity cards for foreign nationals, opposed by the Conservatives, will also help to act as a shield against illegal immigration.

Labour's new Australian-style points-based system for immigrants to the UK is ensuring that only those with the skills the country needs can enter the UK. The points-based system gives the government the ability to flex its approach, so that it can respond to situations such as the recession and business needs, and act accordingly. In contrast, the Conservatives would introduce a rigid cap on immigration, which would not allow the flexibility we need. In addition, to combat the threat of terrorism, the new passenger screening system will identify high-risk individuals, screening 95 per cent of all passengers and crew by December 2010 and 100 per cent by March 2014.

Labour's earned citizenship proposals will also mean that migrants are required to speak English, work hard, pay tax and support themselves without access to benefits or social housing until they have earned citizenship. Newcomers who break the law are also being removed at record levels.

I believe that migrants make a great contribution to the UK economy, and that on the whole managed migration enriches our local communities. The Treasury estimated that new migrants contributed £6 billion to the economy in 2006.

Opportunity communities

While the government invests money in home building, policing and protecting our borders, we know this investment is not enough unless we can also invest in opportunities, particularly for young people. Young people need opportunities to try new things and learn new skills in order to flourish – and indeed, if young people can access these opportunities they are less likely to get involved in the crime or anti-social behaviour that can plague our communities.

Regeneration means more than jobs, it also means access to arts, culture and sports for everyone in the community. Labour made access to museums free in 1997, and is subsidising theatre for the young so that everyone, including in homes where money is tight, has the opportunity to enjoy the things that make our lives more varied and fulfilled.

The London Olympics are an opportunity to raise the aspirations and broaden the horizons of more people, with the Youth Olympics, Cultural Olympics and the recent introduction of free swimming for young people and pensioners.

Steve, Chief Executive, Interplay Community Theatre, Leeds

Over the past decade we have experienced unprecedented demand for the work of our charity, which provides film, theatre and music opportunities for young people. I believe that this increase is directly attributable to the government's investment in the arts.

> Because of government funding we are working with young people using film as a tool of engagement and we are working in schools as part of Creative Partnerships. We have been able to set up and run the I Love West Leeds festival, a community arts initiative that has been a vehicle for renewal and celebration. We have valued this support both locally and nationally.

The voluntary sector, including community theatres like Steve's, is often more knowledgeable about local need and more responsive to people's individual circumstances. A fourth-term Labour government would look to work even more with the voluntary sector to provide opportunities, especially for young people.

Under Labour the voluntary sector has already grown rapidly – by 2008 the income of British charities was £48.4 billion, more than double what it was in 1997. This reflects the extraordinary generosity of the British public, demonstrated most recently through the donations to Haiti via the Disasters Emergency Committee, but has also been helped by supportive government policies, such as dropping the Conservatives' £600 minimum Gift Aid donation threshold, allowing charities to claim back more money. Labour has also supported charities through the recession with £60 million to help volunteers, charities and social enterprises.

David Cameron talks about setting the voluntary sector free to flourish, but what does it mean in practice? Even the largest charity in Leeds West, with a turnover of £2 million, receives the vast majority of its funding from central and local government – including grants to deliver drug treatment services, youth projects and family support. In Leeds West, average earnings are only £16,000. Although we have social enterprises – a community cafe, an arts festival, a gardening business and a new business supporting older people to stay in their homes – the local voluntary sector does not have the capacity to be independent of government. The voluntary sector will not flourish without partnership and cannot do all that it does through donations and local goodwill alone – especially in poorer neighbourhoods.

Too often the Conservatives attack Britain and do us down, with David Cameron claiming that the state has somehow 'squeezed out kindness' from our society. But the British give the second highest amount to charity in the world (0.73 per cent of GDP), and more than one in four adults volunteer on a regular basis. The slogan 'broken Britain' ignores the fact that in most of our neighbourhoods people do look out for each other – young people are respectful and hard-working and the vast majority of parents do their very best for their children. But this reality does not fit Cameron's rhetoric. We should be proud of the work of community activists and the voluntary sector, but realistic about the partnership needed to truly empower people and communities.

Diverse communities

Labour's vision is for a fair, inclusive society where there is opportunity for everyone regardless of gender, disability, sexual orientation, age, race, religion or belief. From challenging disability discrimination to tackling the pay gap, to fighting racism and introducing civil partnerships, Labour has been at the forefront of change.

Gurinder Chadha, director of *Bend it Like Beckham* and *It's a Wonderful Afterlife*

I will be supporting Labour in these elections as I always have and as my parents have before me. I grew up in Southall, West London, as the daughter of immigrants who both worked hard, but struggled in the face of prejudice and often violence at the hand of right-wing racists. The 1980s under Thatcher were a terrible time for people like my family with a government who believed in unemployment to increase poverty and break the spirit of ordinary working people by peddling jingoistic nonsense about Britain.

Well, I wanted to do something about it and hence I became a journalist, then a director, to show the world the Britain that I live in and love – the Britain of today and the future as I show in my films.

I have got to know Gordon and Sarah Brown because of their huge support of the films, arts and culture of Britain. I have been invited to Downing Street as a cultural representative of our nation – something my parents would never have imagined in those early days of struggle.

I believe Gordon and Sarah really share the same values of those of us who believe in a sense of community spirit and civil responsibility for all our citizens, not just those who can afford more. The Britain I will vote for is one where all cultures, races and religions are respected and we work to build on the cultural successes and diversity we have achieved and continue to show to other countries. I believe the Labour Party and Gordon Brown will do that with hard work, sincerity and passion.

Britain is more tolerant and diverse than ever before and legislation reflects the changing values of modern Britain.

The Conservative Party's record on equality is poor. They opposed the repeal of Section 28 (which made it illegal to teach homosexuality as acceptable), although even after repeal some Conservative councils still tried to avoid making changes. They opposed Labour's action in lowering the age of consent for homosexual couples, and have fought numerous general election campaigns focused on stirring up hatred and fear about immigration.

Judith, Glasgow

This Labour government has done more for gay equality than any other government in British history. It's because of this government that my wife and I were able not just to access the same rights as straight married couples, but also to have our relationship marked and celebrated by our family and friends. When your relationship is consistently ignored and belittled, the importance of the dignity of legal recognition cannot be over-stated.

It's this Labour government that's made it illegal for us to be discriminated against. It's this Labour government that has changed the law on adoption to make it possible for us to jointly adopt, so hopefully we'll be able to offer a loving, secure childhood to children who've had an extremely tough start in life.

Making a lifelong commitment to each other has brought a new level of stability and happiness to our home. For us, it's meant the beginning of a new family.

Proud and strong communities

Britain is not broken – it is full of opportunities, yet there is still work to do to ensure that every family and community can make the most of these opportunities. But we should be honest about our strengths too. More people give to charity and volunteer, community groups offer football practice, rugby clubs, local radio stations, summer fayres, book clubs and community festivals. London is hosting the Olympics because of our diversity, culture, heritage and future. And the vast majority of us are proud to be British and proud of the places where we live. This is not a country on its knees, whatever the Conservatives try to tell us. It is a country that has come out of the recession fighting, ready to meet the challenges and opportunities ahead.

Restoring trust in politics

Britain faces many challenges in the next few years: building a more sustainable economy; ensuring that everyone has access to excellent, local, schools and hospitals; investing in strong and sustainable communities; and tackling climate change. What these challenges have in common is that they won't be addressed by government acting alone. A partnership is needed and partnerships require trust.

The abuse of expenses by some MPs has tarnished the reputation of all politicians. To restore trust, MPs, through their actions and behaviour, must demonstrate they are worthy of the office they hold. Unless trust is restored and integrity upheld, it will be difficult, if not impossible, to address the challenges that confront us.

At the election, I am standing to be the MP for Leeds West and it is local people who will decide whom they send to Parliament and who will judge their MP on his or her record. The constituency link means every part of the country is represented in Westminster. But an MP will only be able to make a difference if they have the respect of local people.

To restore trust, there must be much greater transparency. I have pledged to publish my expenses on a monthly basis. Constituents must be able to judge whether claims are legitimate and whether they represent good value for money. If an MP does abuse the system their constituents should have the power to recall them by means of a ballot.

There must also be greater clarity on what MPs are entitled to claim for. Being an MP requires you to spend time in two places

– with the travel and housing costs that entails. It also requires casework, surgeries, meetings and visits in the constituency – and an MP will need staff and an office to help them do that.

But while MPs must only claim for what they need to do their job, it is important that people are not deterred from standing for Parliament because it is too expensive or incompatible with bringing up a family. It would be a hugely retrograde step if Parliament was to become the preserve of the rich, or if women or people with young families did not put themselves forward.

More than 130 MPs have already announced that they are standing down at the next election, and it is likely that this number will increase. Whatever the outcome of the election, there will be a huge change in the membership of the House of Commons this year. The 2010 intake has a responsibility to restore trust and build a system that inspires confidence.

But beyond preventing the scandal of duck houses, moats and plasma televisions, we need a new constitutional settlement to give people more say over how Britain is run. This should include reform of the House of Lords; a referendum on the voting system; more devolution to the regions and communities of the UK; greater engagement of young people; better scrutiny of legislation; and more time to debate bills in Parliament. These reforms would increase accountability and engagement. They would also ensure that decisions better reflect the will of the people.

Without reform, cynicism will prevail and people will further disengage – politics would be poorer as a result. It is the responsibility of politicians, from all parties, to show they are worthy of elected office and it is only when trust is restored that MPs can do the things that they were elected to achieve.

So why vote Labour?

As this book has set out, we face an important choice at the next election. It is a choice about what sort of economy we want to build in the wake of the recession – whether we want a government that takes a lead in regulating the banks and investing in the jobs and skills of the future, or one that leaves it to the market to decide. It is also a choice about our schools, hospitals and police – whether we want to make them more personalised to our needs, with guarantees about what we can expect, or whether we are happy to have different standards of care depending on where you live or how much money you have.

Tracey's moving story about discovering she had cancer shows that when we most need support the NHS is there for us. Investment and patient guarantees, introduced by Labour, are ensuring that people like Tracey are treated without delay, saving lives and giving us, and our families, the peace of mind that we need. Ben's story about the transformation of his old primary school shows how far schools have come in the last thirteen years. Gone are the mobile classrooms and pre-fab huts in the playground, replaced by new classrooms, more teachers and teaching assistants and new computer technologies. Ben's little brother is benefiting from that change. The Conservatives opposed the one penny increase in National Insurance to fund NHS spending, opposed Labour's patient guarantees – including to see a cancer specialist within two weeks – and opposed Labour's reforms to make it compulsory for young people to stay in education, training or an apprenticeship until the age of eighteen. The stories of this book show that politics can make a difference and that there is a choice between the policies and priorities of the different parties.

We know that the recession hit British families and businesses hard and that we must build a new economy in the wake of the financial crisis. But Kelly's story shows how the government has supported families through the recession, rather than leaving people to fend for themselves and risking condemning a generation of young people to the scrapheap as happened in the recessions of the past. Economists estimate that unemployment has risen by 500,000 fewer than if the government had have pursued the discredited Conservative approach of the 1980s and 1990s. Kelly's family have been protected by support from the Labour government and businesses like Phil's in Leeds have also been supported through the recession. And yet, every measure that Labour has taken during the recession has been opposed by David Cameron and George Osborne.

We face a choice at the election about what sort of country and society we want Britain to be and what sort of change we want to see. It is Labour who will extend opportunities to families on modest and middle incomes and it is Labour who will help more people fulfil their ambitions and aspirations. The Labour Party recognises that to make the change we need a government which does not just leave the economy and public services to market forces, but instead helps correct the excesses of markets – so that they serve people and not just profits. I hope that after reading this book you will vote Labour and I hope that you will come away believing that politics does matter, that voting matters and that together we can make a difference.